D0570433

Dancing
in the Kitchen

Colleen Duffy-Someck

Copyright © 2016 by Colleen Duffy-Someck

Cover photo by Shawn Peterson of Peterson Portraits
Back cover and recipe photos by Sara Someck

The information contained herein is for educational purposes only and is not meant to diagnose, prescribe, or treat any condition. This information should not be used as a substitute for medical counseling with a qualified professional.

All rights reserved. No part of this book may be used or reproduced by any means, graphic, electronic, or mechanical, including photocopying, recording, taping or by any information storage retrieval system without the written permission of the author except in the case of brief quotations embodied in critical articles and reviews.

LifeRich Publishing is a registered trademark of The Reader's Digest Association, Inc.

LifeRich Publishing books may be ordered through booksellers or by contacting:

LifeRich Publishing
1663 Liberty Drive
Bloomington, IN 47403
www.liferichpublishing.com
1 (888) 238-8637

Because of the dynamic nature of the Internet, any web addresses or links contained in this book may have changed since publication and may no longer be valid. The views expressed in this work are solely those of the author and do not necessarily reflect the views of the publisher, and the publisher hereby disclaims any responsibility for them.

ISBN: 978-1-4897-0689-8 (softcover)
ISBN: 978-1-4897-0690-4 (hardcover)

Library of Congress Control Number: 2016901629

Printed in the USA.

LifeRich Publishing rev. date: 4/8/2016

contents

preface

Before the words were born onto the pages that would become my book, I knew what the title would be. I spend a lot of time in the kitchen preparing food for my family and friends, and I realized one day that I actually dance while I'm cooking. Standing in front of the stove, I move two steps to the right to stir my pot of beans. Remembering I need carrots, I twirl and take three steps forward to get to the refrigerator. With a half turn and two steps to the left, I arrive at the sink to wash the carrots. With each day and each delicious meal, a different dance is created.

Sometimes when we dance, we have a partner. It's important to watch, feel, and follow each other's steps so that together our rhythms are one, creating a beautiful dance. The image that comes to mind when I think about dancing in the kitchen is a connected and conscious dance between our bodies and food, preparing and eating healthy nourishing meals with balance and awareness. Following the leads of hunger and fullness can guide our steps in a graceful dance with food.

I don't recall how many times I've heard or used the phrase, "dancing through life." Just like dancing to music, we each hear our own life's tune. We maneuver our way through the years with a style and rhythm that aren't quite the same as anyone else's. So my story is about my life's dance, as it twisted and turned through twenty years of an eating disorder to eventually find healing through dancing in the kitchen.

Dancing is so personal. It is an expression of the soul. The way we move when we hear music is unique to each and every one of us. How we hear the music and the way it makes us feel determine how we move our bodies to express our uniqueness. But let's say that you want to learn a particular type of dance, so you take lessons. Once your dance moves are perfected and you know them by heart, you can add slight variations to make it your own. This cookbook is meant to share some of my cooking "moves" with you. My goal is to help you build a foundation of preparing foods in a way that may be more nourishing and healthy. My hope is that once you learn my recipes, you will find the confidence to add your personal touch, making each recipe your own. By adding your own flare, you will make them ideal for you and your family's taste buds. Cooking, like movement, is an expression of the soul and a way to nourish the spirit.

The recipes here encourage flexibility and experimentation. You choose a recipe, learn how it's made, and then make it your own. I give you the basic steps, and once you feel comfortable, you have the freedom to add your own personal twist. Play and have fun preparing your own dishes. Cooking to feed yourself and those you love is a lovely dance, a dance that is definitely worth learning. It is my honor to share my story and recipes with you in hopes that they may show you a new way of dancing in the kitchen.

Part 1: My Story

Life is a journey, not a destination. It's not about the arrival but all that is learned in the process of getting there. I believe that it is important to keep this adage in mind, and I remind myself of these wise words daily.

I don't consider myself religious. Spiritual? Yes. Some days I wish I were more spiritually evolved than I am now. When I reflect upon where I was thirty years ago, I sometimes don't recognize the person I was. I have made so many changes over the years that my memories can feel like figments of my imagination. Today, I am so different—mentally and emotionally—from the person I was before I embarked on a twenty-year journey at the age of eighteen. And yet, the experiences of my life are lessons that brought me to where I am today, right here, right now.

This is my story. Some, whose paths have intersected with mine, may weave a different tale of the experiences we shared because their view of these events is seen through their eyes, not mine. So to those of you who know me, I say, this is how I perceived my life through my eyes and mine alone.

dancing in the kitchen

Have you ever had an "ah-ha!" moment about something that happened years earlier? You realize you missed something really big in your perception of the event. I had a very big "ah-ha!" moment when I started writing this story.

My childhood was rough. I didn't have many friends, was teased a lot, and wandered rather aimlessly through my preteen years. I was born in the middle of eleven children, and even though I had many siblings around me, I felt lonely and lost. I don't have many memories of these years except one, one that changed my life forever.

In 1972, I celebrated my twelfth birthday. I had invited a few girls over for my party, and we were eating cake and opening gifts when my mom called to me. "Hey, I think I see something in the backyard." I looked through the sliding glass doors that opened up to our backyard and didn't see anything unusual, so I went back to opening presents. I heard her voice again. "Why don't you go outside and see what that is?" Unwillingly, I went to the door and still saw nothing. My friends encouraged me to step outside, and when I did, my life changed forever.

Outside was a beautiful chestnut-colored horse. *Was this horse for me?* As I looked into the faces of everyone standing there with me in the yard, their expressions told me the answer was "yes!" My parents had bought me a horse for my birthday! MY PARENTS HAD BOUGHT ME A HORSE!!! I ran to the mare and couldn't wait to get on her. I adjusted the saddle, put my foot in the stirrup, and pulled myself up and into the tack. I rode around our yard like a queen while everyone cheered! *Was this really happening to me? Was she really mine?* I was so full of joy, and I couldn't remember a time that I was happier. I had been taking riding lessons but never thought in a million years that I would have a horse of my own.

This mare, Mecca, became my confidant, my best friend, and my teacher. I loved her so much! As the years went by and I became a teen, my love for Mecca grew deeper and stronger. I spent many hours riding her bareback in the fields behind our house, never tiring of her company. Mecca and I became one when we were together. I could ride with just the twine from a bale of hay around her neck, and we would travel for miles. All I needed to do was think about where I wanted to go, and Mecca would just know where to take me. To this day, I don't know how we communicated. What I do know is we understood each other so well, we were so free together, and we had a heart-to-heart connection.

I sold Mecca when I was almost eighteen, knowing that I would be going to college soon. I don't remember saying goodbye, and this omission still haunts me. I didn't hug her or tell her how much I loved her or how much she meant to me. The next day, after the trailer had picked her up and hauled her to her new home, I realized I'd made a huge mistake. I felt as though a piece of my heart had been ripped away. I felt physical pain in my chest. I pulled out a piece of paper from my pocket and dialed the phone number written on it. A woman answered, and I told her I wanted to buy Mecca back. When she said that Mecca had already been sold to someone else, my heart sank. What does a seventeen-year-old know about the consequences of living without her best friend? Mecca had been such a huge part of my life, and now I was all alone, again.

I tucked my precious memories of Mecca into a small, protected place in my heart. She lives there now, and I often think about her and the gifts she gave me. She offered me her unconditional love. I knew she loved me; she was always there for me. Where does one find a friend like that? This was my first experience with a deep and connected love. Many years later, Mecca still wields her magic because, you see, she lives within me.

In 2012, I started writing this cookbook, and as I struggled with where to begin, the story of Mecca seemed to flow out of nowhere, filling up the pages on the computer. Then my "ah- ha!" moment struck. Growing up in a large family doesn't guarantee that you will never feel alone because I felt lonely often. I believed that I didn't matter to anyone. I thought no one loved me, not even my parents. As a teen, I had a rocky relationship with my mother. Not that I was a bad kid or that she was a bad mom but we just didn't get along. For many, many years I had placed this feeling of being unlovable in a deep place at the core of my being.

As I wrote on a rainy winter evening, the story of Mecca and my childhood appeared on the pages. Mecca had once again worked her magic. For the first time in forty years, as I read the words I had typed, I had a revelation: My parents *had* loved me. They *had* recognized my preteen pain. To help me through a difficult time, they had bought me a horse, a companion to spend time with and someone to love. I felt so ashamed at not seeing what they had provided for me until that moment. For forty years, I had been unable to see their deep love and concern for me, even though it had been there all along. At that moment my soul began to heal, as I finally comprehended my parents' love for me.

I called my parents the next day and could barely get the words out through my uncontrollable tears. I told them how thankful I was for their understanding and for what they'd done for me. I apologized for not realizing this sooner and said I regretted that it had taken years to understand their love for me. On this journey called life, messages are revealed when one is ready to receive them, and for some, it can take decades to fully understand. For all of us, it's important to trust and enjoy the ride.

So, what does my story have to do with dancing in the kitchen? Not long after I sold Mecca and went off to college, I developed an eating disorder. Even though I didn't know what to do with my life after high school, I went to college because that's what everyone did. I'd had a rough time making friends in high school, and college was no different. I felt like I didn't fit in, and as the months passed, I became more and more reclusive. My dorm wasn't on campus because of an overflow of students; it was about ten miles away. There weren't as many girls in this particular dorm, and everyone had their own room. I spent a lot of time alone, feeling that nobody wanted to spend time with me and that I wasn't good enough to have any friends. So I focused on something that was familiar to me: food.

I'd been interested in natural foods from a very early age. When I was twelve, my mom urged me and my siblings to stop eating candy and chips and drinking soda, after she'd seen Adele Davis on television. This advice resonated with me, so I did as she suggested. I don't remember missing any of these foods. My hungry mind ate up any and all information about eating healthy.

In college, I wanted to continue eating healthy foods, so I prepared my own meals in the dorm's kitchen. In hindsight, I can see how this choice created separation between me and the other women in my dorm. Sharing meals together was a time for bonding, and I missed out on that.

During my first semester of college, I gained some weight, which my brother noticed when I went home for winter break. I committed myself to starting a diet at the beginning of the new year, after all of the holiday celebrations were over. I followed a fat-free diet and took up running. Eating whole grains, salads, fresh fruit, and low-fat yogurt practically melted the unwanted weight from my body. In one month, I dropped 15 pounds, and with it, I lost my period. The new me felt invincible! I had set a goal for myself and achieved it. I felt in control of my life. I was running three to six miles per day and eating healthy. I had never felt better. Until everything fell apart.

In May, I went home for my brother's confirmation, and there was a party afterward in the church hall. Some elderly women had placed cakes and cookies on the tables. There were plates and plates of them. I figured that since I hadn't eaten any sugar in months, it wouldn't hurt to have just one cookie. But was I wrong! I ate one cookie, then two cookies, then cake, and then more cake. I felt as if someone had jumped into my body and taken control of me. I didn't stop eating the desserts until I was so stuffed that I could barely move. That night, I fell asleep with horrible stomach pains while trying to comprehend what had happened to me at the church. I slept fitfully.

When morning came, I boarded the bus back to school. I told myself that the binging was a random indiscretion and that I would get back on track with my healthy eating. It was a new day, and I put what happened the day before behind me. Little did I know how wrong that assessment was. This was the beginning of a full-on eating disorder that I would struggle with for years, as I tried to stabilize and create a healthy relationship with food. So the battle began to control my out-of-control eating, and eventually, I lost all direction and momentum on my quest for a healthy relationship with food.

In general, I ate well, continuing with my fat- and sugar-free diet. Sometimes, when I was offered something sweet and rich, I would find that I had no willpower to resist the temptation. If I decided to indulge myself in a delicacy, I would eat it uncontrollably. Then, to offset the binge, I would run extra miles or fast from food for a day or two. I had deemed certain foods, mostly anything with sugar or fat, as "unhealthy." If I even tasted any of these items, it would lead to a binge. The conversations in my head were never-ending, "Eat this, not that. Eat it! Don't eat it! Yes! No!" The mental chatter was exhausting, and I was exhausted. I felt out of control, with not a minute of peace in my life. The constant conversations had taken the place of that invincibility I'd once felt. Even without the binges, my life was an uncomfortable one, and my relationship with food was a constant battle.

Months went by and then a year, as I continued having ups and downs with food. I gained some weight and lost some weight, drifting along with no direction or purpose. The summer after my sophomore year of college, my parents and I agreed that I would go to Sweden and work at a roadside inn called Kungshaga Hotell. My parents had met the family who owned the hotel, and after a conversation with them, it was agreed that I would work there for the summer. Because of my interest in food, my parents thought it would be good for me to work in a commercial kitchen preparing food for the hotel guests.

However, as the time drew near for me to fly to Sweden, I changed my mind. I really didn't want to leave home, but because the plans had been made and I had my ticket, I didn't tell anyone how I felt.

A week before my scheduled flight, I was feeling very depressed about my life. I recall feeling so low that I contemplated suicide. I sat outside on the grass in my parents' backyard and planned how I would do it. Then I cried and cried until there were no tears left. Luckily, I became so afraid that I couldn't go through with it. So I moped around until the day arrived to leave for Sweden. As I boarded the plane for Stockholm, I turned myself on "auto pilot," shut down all my emotions, and flew into the unknown.

Once in Orsa, where Kungshaga Hotell was, I missed home and wanted to go back. I called and begged my parents to allow me to come home. "No, you have to stay the three months as planned," Mom said. I was miserable and depressed. I turned my focus inward and went on a very strict diet of salad, apples, and Wasa crackers. I also ran two to three miles a day. The diet gave me something else to focus on other than wanting to go home; it gave me a purpose.

Before I started my diet, I had gained about ten pounds within the first couple of weeks of my arrival in Sweden. None of my clothes fit me, so I'd purchased a pair of baggy, purple pants in Orsa that I wore every day.

On July 1st, I started my diet. About two weeks later, my purple pants were dirty, so I needed something else to wear. I dug into my suitcase and pulled out a pair of jeans. I put them on and was shocked. In two weeks' time, I'd lost 15 pounds! I grabbed the extra fabric on the jeans and felt proud of the results of my dieting.

I continued my regimen of eating minimal calories until I met my mother in Europe six weeks later. We would be traveling around Germany and Italy for a couple of weeks, and then I would take the train back to Sweden to finish out the summer. I was so relieved to be with my mom that in the time we spent together, I gained back all of the weight I'd lost. I wasn't binging, just eating anything I wanted. I had starved myself for weeks, and now I could celebrate that my mom and I were together and having so much fun. When the time came for me to go back to Orsa, I convinced my mom to let me go home with her. I did not want to go back to Sweden. Fortunately, we found a reasonably priced ticket back to the United States. I was going home!

Once I returned, I felt so guilty over gaining all of the weight back that I started another diet, and the roller coaster ride continued.

I quit college at the beginning of my junior year and went to work for a health food restaurant in St. Paul, Minnesota called Good Earth. It was a great job, and I made good money as a waitress. It was here, while living in St. Paul, that I learned about the macrobiotic diet after reading an article in a magazine. I took cooking classes and read a lot of books to learn more about the macrobiotic philosophy. I was drawn to this way of life and the control that the diet offered me. There were a lot of rules to follow, which I was actually pretty good at. Although I loved the food and the macrobiotic way of life, my eating disorder wasn't improving. I weighed the least I had in a very long time. I was stick-thin and cold all the time.

As my binges increased, my self-esteem sank. Looking back, I don't think I would have survived had I stayed in Minnesota. In addition to cutting calories and over exercising, I had learned how to make myself throw up to help me manage my weight. I now had many destructive tools under my belt to keep weight off my body: running, fasting, and purging, all to an extreme. Although it is hard to look back sometimes, I have to remember that life is a journey. To this day, despite the difficult struggles and mental anguish, I wouldn't change any of these experiences. They have made me into who I am today.

While my health continued its downward spiral, a force outside of me was pulling in the direction of California. I was visiting a friend in San Diego for a couple of weeks when I decided that California would be a great place to live. From there, every possible door opened, paving the way for me to move west and leave my family, my job, and all that I had known. I lined up a waitressing job at another Good Earth restaurant just east of San Diego and felt very lucky to be able to transfer. I also found a woman who needed a roommate to share her one-bedroom apartment. It was expensive, but it was also one block from the beach. It didn't matter to me that I'd be sleeping on the couch. I had a place to live and a job.

I flew back to Minnesota filled with hope for a new beginning. I would be leaving my pain and sorrows behind and starting a new life where no one knew me. I forgot one thing, that ultimate truth: "No matter where you go, there you are." My move to California marked the beginning of finding myself.

Once all the loose ends were tied up in Minnesota, I packed everything I owned into my Le Car and drove solo across the United States, anxious to see what was in store for me. It was a three-day journey that would bring me to a new home in California and eventually to a home that I discovered inside of me.

Despite living in a new and beautiful state, my radical and painful eating habits continued. I tried with all I had to figure out why I wasn't "normal" like everyone else. I had what I called "good" days and "bad" days. Good days meant no binging, no purging, and eating inside the dietary restrictions I'd set for myself. My "do not eat" list now included dairy, eggs, flour products, and meat. If I ate any of these foods, it would instigate a binge, followed by a purge.

After living in San Diego for a year, I quit my job at Good Earth and moved into a macrobiotic center called Grain Country, where I had been volunteering once a week. My job consisted of prepping and cooking foods in their restaurant kitchen. I lived with a group of men and women who also worked at the center. I was looking forward to not being alone.

It was there, in the kitchen of Grain Country, that I discovered my gift. Up until then, I didn't believe that I had a gift or a purpose, but one day, it revealed itself to me: cooking. I felt so at home in the kitchen, and I realized I loved all the aspects of creating nourishing meals. I had held the belief that I needed a college degree to "be someone" in the world, but I soon realized that holding a diploma wasn't necessary for me. I discovered that the kitchen of Grain Country would be my classroom, and I would be its student. I was ready!

Creating tasty food for health and longevity can be challenging. Back then, preparing macrobiotic dishes that "normal" Americans would want to eat was a difficult task because the food is, quite simply, unlike most American food. I found that, because I had pretty balanced taste buds, I could put together vegetables, beans, grains, or seaweed, and *ta-da*, the food tasted quite delicious. After working at Grain Country for a few months, I became the manager of the kitchen when a good friend of mine left the management job and moved back east. I had more responsibility, but I loved every minute of it. I was also in charge of the weekly cooking classes, and I enjoyed that, too! I felt wonderful teaching people how to prepare healthy food. I loved knowing that my students would go home and prepare foods that would improve their health and the health of their families. I remember calling my parents and telling them how fulfilling it was to teach these cooking classes and how I felt so at home. I was thrilled. The restaurant was getting busier, and we were selling out of special dinner meals that I created. Each day I spent in the kitchen was filling up a hole that had been inside me for so long. Little by little I was gaining confidence that I was good at something. I would have this "high" feeling every so often, but most of the time, I felt just mediocre. I tried to convince myself that I was worthy of goodness. Even though it didn't always work, I knew that I was beginning to see myself differently.

Mind you, my dysfunction with food was still alive and well. It was at Grain Country where I heard the words that would be one of the keys to my recovery. David Jackson, the owner of the center, shared his wisdom after I confided in him about my shame over binging and purging. He suggested that I begin to view the binging and purging in another way. Even though I was overeating and making myself throw up less often, I still viewed my cup as half-empty instead of half-full. I thought that if I lost control, binged, and then purged even for one day, I was a failure. I thought I had to be perfect. David helped me to recognize my successes and to celebrate them, to acknowledge these victories and the strides I was making. There's a secret here that I will share with you but not just yet.

Months of living in San Diego turned into years, and I slowly put the found pieces of myself back together, rebuilding the real me—the me that had fragmented so many years ago. Being constantly aware of what was causing me to flip from my so-called "normal eating" to binging and purging was an all-encompassing and downright exhausting task. But my "spells" were getting further and further apart. There was still a lot of work to do, but as David said, I was getting better, and I believed him.

After being at Grain Country for almost a year, I met this amazing man named Jimbo. He owned a health food store called Jimbo's…Naturally!, which was just down the street from Grain Country. He and I started dating, and I felt so lucky to have such a special person in my life, someone who wanted to spend time with me and enjoyed my company. So when it finally dawned on me that he really cared about me, that strange, dark voice living in my mind spoke up and said, "You're not worthy." This voice set out to sabotage something good that was happening in my life.

How could Jimbo like me? I wasn't perfect, and I had loads of baggage. I still binged and purged, so what could this kind and generous man possibly see in me? I was so far from perfect. I still didn't have a healthy self-image, so I couldn't wrap my head around the fact that Jimbo liked me. Emotionally, I tried to push him away because I felt so uncomfortable with all of the attention he was giving me. But you know what? He stayed. He stayed by my side through all of my rough patches, my ups and downs, my ins and outs. Every step of the way, Jimbo was there for me. He was my rock, never wavering in his love for me. He believed in me. He was the person that I couldn't be for myself. At least, not yet.

Now I really wanted to get well, so I set out to find as many of the broken pieces of myself as I could. In the process, I searched for something more that might help me end my eating disorder. I was yearning to shut this dysfunction down and be done with it once and for all. I had heard about OA, Overeaters Anonymous. OA is similar to AA but addresses food addiction instead of alcohol issues. I went to some meetings and felt that this would be the perfect program for me. The OA approach consists of eating three "normal" meals a day, with no snacking in between. I would finally have a way to control my binges! I could eat anything I wanted for my meals as long as it was a normal portion.

So I started eating foods I'd once considered "unhealthy." I ate yogurt and granola, muffins, eggs, and cookies. I gave myself permission to eat anything I wanted. It was the first time in years that I set aside my strict and harsh dietary rules to focus on just the meal before me. Any food that I craved and hadn't eaten in a long time, I would have at one of my three regular meals. I felt a new sense of freedom—freedom from the thoughts that once had bounced around in my head and freedom from figuring out which foods were "good" or "bad." Three months went by, and my life seemed to be going fabulously well. No binging, no purging! No constant arguments in my head. Great! Little did I know that the last layer of the onion was about to reveal itself to me. I had asked for a complete healing, and I was finally about to get what I asked for.

* * *

Every summer I go back to Wisconsin to visit my family, and this particular summer was no different. One day, about a half-hour after lunch, my mom asked me to go down to a local restaurant to have tea and share a piece of pie. I thought, *Oh no! I'd love to go have pie, but I already had my lunch, and I'm not supposed to eat again until dinner.* I told her this, and her response turned out to be the second key to my recovery. She shared her thoughts on how she sees all these rules as controlling and confining, not freeing. How could I experience freedom with food if there was so much control around it? How could I not go and eat pie when that's what I wanted to do? So I went and shared a piece of pie with my mom, and it was delicious. I broke the rules, and my world didn't come crashing down. Wow!

My mom had pointed me toward the door where the last piece of my recovery would be found. I turned the knob, walked through the door, and knew she was right! I didn't want to be controlled by the endless rules, the dos and don'ts, around food anymore. Much of my life had been controlled by when to do this and when to do that. I wanted to be FREE!! How was I going to do this on my own? There weren't any self-help books on being free from food addiction, and I did look. I realized I would have to walk this path alone and put to rest this demon that had been a part of me for what was, by now, way too long. I wanted my self back, my whole self, my free self. How would I begin, and what would I do?

I recalled a saying I'd seen somewhere: "The journey of a thousand miles begins with the first step." As I took my first step, the door closed behind me. It was time to unlock the chains and be set free.

My rule? No rules! All food is allowed. No "good" food, no "bad" food. I stay in touch with my feelings of hunger and fullness. My goal is to be healthy. I want to eat healthy food, but I also want the liberty to eat any food I want, whenever I choose. This is the goal: I want to be free. Freedom for me means no restrictions on food choices. My most important commitment to myself is to be mentally present when I eat. Whenever I eat a food that was previously on my "do not eat" list, I do my best to share the item.

I love cappuccinos and croissants. Previously, when I allowed myself to splurge on these two delicacies, the indulgence would trigger a binge. Now I set my armor aside before walking into a coffee shop to order these previously off-limits foods. I find a table and sit down to enjoy my purchases, all the while remaining very aware and present. I savor every bite and every sip, feeling satisfied physically and emotionally.

I practiced with these two foods before moving on to my next test: going into the coffee shop and buying any pastry and coffee drink that appealed to me. I stayed in touch with everything that was happening to me mentally and physically. *Was I sensitive to the caffeine today? Was half of my drink enough to satisfy me for this visit? How about the croissant or treat? When was I satisfied with its deliciousness and able to walk out, leaving the remaining bites resting in the trash can?*

This was working! I was gaining confidence in my ability to stop eating when I was satisfied. I just had to stay present and be aware of my experience. Mind you, there were still some slip-ups, but my life was no longer run by rules and endless debates in my head.

One evening, Jimbo suggested going to dinner at a local all-you-can-eat soup and salad restaurant with our two children. I was very tired and didn't feel like cooking, so I agreed. While there, I felt a binge coming on, that overwhelming urge to continue eating even though I felt full. I had come to realize that when I was tired, it was easier for me to slip into a binge, and tonight was no different. I ate too much! I was stuffed! I felt uncomfortable! When I got home I mustered up the nerve to throw up my dinner. When I looked into the toilet, I saw red! I had no idea if it was blood, the kidneys beans from my salad, or the beets. It didn't matter. This experience was enough to put a halt to my purging for good. I was done and wanted this to be the last time. And it was.

Even though purging had come to a sudden end, my quest to eat "normally" continued. My friend Susan and I would often go to a local bakery/restaurant for lunch. We would always order a dessert to split. I felt satisfied emotionally with my friend and physically with my food. I would create new challenges for myself and, most of the time, accomplish them. Sometimes I'd eat a bit too much and would feel fuller than I wanted to be, but I stuck with my commitment to never purge again.

Years went by, and one day I awoke filled with so much gratitude. I realized it had been years since I'd binged or purged. How could this be? It seemed like just yesterday the emotional eating and the endless conversations in my head around food were such a large part of my life. At some point during the past few years, I'd said goodbye to the dark spirit that had made its home inside my head. I contemplated whether I could say that I had actually recovered from my eating disorder, and I realized the answer was "yes!" I stood tall and proud and said, "YES!" I had created a healthy relationship with food! This particular journey consumed almost twenty years of my life, and through it all, I learned so much about myself. I have come to better understand myself physically, mentally, and emotionally, and on the way, I found the me that I lost so many years ago as a child.

Jimbo and I have four beautiful children: Joshua, Michael, Noah, and Sara, all of who have been a part of my process and witnesses to my journey. I am grateful to each of them for their love and support.

Four years ago, Sara started begging for horseback riding lessons after going on several pony rides while visiting family back in Wisconsin. I thought she would forget about the ponies once we got home, but the pleading continued. One day before Christmas, I asked Sara what was on her Christmas list, and she told me all she wanted was horseback riding lessons. I gave in and called a wonderful woman, Diana, who had for many years babysat my boys and also used to teach riding lessons.

I found out that she was still teaching horseback riding and training horses, not more than five minutes from our home. Three days later, Sara was in the saddle having her first lesson. She was beaming! She had been touched by these beautiful animals, and seeing her joy reminded me of someone I knew. Me!

My daughter brought horses back into my life, and I started to ride again. My heart opened up to allow another horse to live in the space right next to Mecca. I'd come full circle, and so much had happened on my way around. I have a life that is so beautiful, and in creating it, I found my way home.

an inside job

Out of the gate, I can tell you that, generally, diets don't work. I've seen many people try the latest fad diet to lose weight. Even when they do, they tend to gain it back. Why? Because it's not about the food as much as it is about lifestyle choices, portion sizes, and your mental state.

I am not here to tell you what foods to eat and what foods not to eat. What I can offer you is my experience and the knowledge that comes from it. As the saying goes, "Hindsight is 20/20."

Looking back, I realize that my recovery took determination and commitment. I had to be willing to do what it would take, I mean WHATEVER it would take, to regain a balanced life. Friends, family, co-workers, and counselors all meant well when they tried to help me with my addiction, but I now know that they couldn't do it for me! I was the only one who held the key to my recovery. I knew myself better than anyone else knew me. If it was to be, it was up to me. Outsiders may have inspired me, guided me, and lectured me, but the work that needed to be done was done by me and only me. I wanted recovery so badly that I never gave up.

Who should love you more than yourself? No one. We spend our lives looking outside of ourselves, looking for someone to love us. But really, how can we recognize love "out there" without knowing and loving ourselves first? You are unique, and there is no one like you in the whole world. So why compare yourself to anyone else if you are so different? It's necessary to love and understand yourself as best you can because you are the only one living in your body. It is up to you to know what your physical, mental, and emotional needs are. If you place your well-being into the hands of others by following what they tell you to do, you're muting the most important voice of all: your own.

I believe that many of us have lost touch with our body's inner wisdom and no longer follow its gentle nudges to bring us back into balance. It's important to understand what's needed to take care of our bodies, so they can last well into old age. Your body knows what's best for it, and it will tell you what it needs. You just have to listen and learn to understand its unique language.

Do you know what triggers you to overeat? What happens to you mentally and emotionally? For me, overeating was often triggered by feeling bad about myself. I would mentally regress and recall voices from my childhood that spoke about how I wasn't good enough, how I was broken, or how I was unlovable. These voices brought back a lot of emotional pain that I wanted to escape from, so I turned to food. I used binging on sweets as an attempt to stuff down those painful memories to become emotionally numb. Once I made the decision to binge, the anticipation of that first bite was exhilarating. When the sugar hit my bloodstream, I felt high. I would continue eating until my stomach was stretched to its limit, creating so much discomfort that my physical pain was louder than the voices in my head. Purging was my way of getting rid of the evidence that I was weak, that I had lost control, and that, once again, I'd given in to the voices in my head. Even though the pain was gone from my stomach, I knew the voices would be back.

Why was this continuing to happen, this vicious circle? I came to realize that my emotionally wounded inner child was trying to protect itself from painful feelings that still ran deep. As a child, I never stood up for myself. I believed everything I was told about myself, which obstructed my view of my *whole* self. Recovery could come only after I addressed these verbal wounds from so long ago, made peace with them, and freed myself from their emotional hold. In order to do this, I found positive statements to replace the damaging ones from the past. I faced, head-on, the suffering of my inner child. No longer would I blindly accept what others said I was or what they told me I couldn't do. I replaced all those negative voices with my voice, my voice speaking of love, inspiration, and possibility.

As each painful emotion revealed itself to me, I chose to feel it, and then let it go, one emotion at a time. It wasn't always easy, and sometimes the old voices were louder than my voice, but over time, they showed up less frequently. I was becoming emotionally stronger, and I didn't need to hide behind food anymore. Letting go of what others thought I was allowed me to become who I thought I could be.

choosing a different path

Let's shift to your story. How do you choose to feed your body? Do you eat on the go? What about waiting until you are so hungry you want to eat everything in sight? Is skipping meals a habit? Do you eat alone when no one can see you? How about at night before bed? Do you eat when you are stressed, angry, or tired? Years ago, I would have answered "yes" to many of these questions.

Right now take a moment to reflect on your relationship with food. Do you live to eat or eat to live? We all need food to survive, and those of us in the United States are lucky to live where food is plentiful. While most Americans don't worry about where their next meal is coming from, some do worry about consuming too much food. Food is practically everywhere we turn, and often not so healthy. With easy accessibility and lower-cost, jumbo-sized packages comes the issue of when and how much to eat. With food always in reach, one must be conscious of why one is eating.

Are you truly hungry, or are you eating because of a restless emotion? Maybe you are sad, lonely, depressed, angry, tired, or bored and not needing any food nourishment at all. If you choose to eat for any of these reasons or any reason other than hunger, this can be considered emotional eating.

love and listen

If you recognize yourself as an emotional eater, I invite you to try a couple of exercises that work for me. It's time to honor your body instead of abusing it. It's time to create a healthy relationship with the body you have.

Exercise #1: Love your body. Your body deserves the utmost respect for all that it does for you. Right now pause and think of three functions your body has taken care of for you today and for which you are thankful. How about your heart beating nonstop? Or maybe your eyes that allow you to see the beauty in a flower or the smile of a friend? Could you, every day, thank your marvelous machine for something it does? Is it fair to your body to abuse it when your emotions become unbalanced? Our physical being is the home of our spirit and should be respected. It's important to bring a new understanding to the body/mind/soul connection because each of these parts makes up the unique you.

Exercise #2: Before you choose to eat, pause. Ask yourself if you are hungry. If you are not, then why do you want to eat? What's going on? I'm not suggesting that you don't eat, but rather, I'm encouraging you to be conscious of why you are eating. If you are tired, can you take a nap? If you are angry, can you talk to a friend about what is bothering you? Would a walk help if you are bored? Instead of running to food, see if you can recognize your patterns, and find something else to do instead of eating. And, if you choose to eat, I have some words of wisdom: quality over quantity.

quality over quantity

Many years ago, when I was pregnant with my first child, I received acupuncture treatments from a Chinese practitioner. He made a suggestion that I will always cherish. He told me that if I had any cravings, I shouldn't ignore them but instead find the best quality of what I wanted and eat it until I felt satisfied. I believe that his words of wisdom played a part in my recovery, and I have shared them with many friends. I practice his advice regularly.

When I'm in an emotional place, and I want something "different," like food that I consider a treat, I think about what I want and then find the best quality of that item. I take the time to sit and really enjoy the flavor, texture, smell, and sensation of my food choice. I listen to how my body is feeling as I eat. This is what I call "eating consciously." I take my time, and I experience no guilt as I savor every bite. I know this thought process works, but it may take some practice to apply it regularly. For those of you who are used to stuffing down without tasting, this will be a transition. All you have to do is pay attention. I believe in you, and I know you can do it! And remember, it's always fun to share with a friend.

the "better than" theory

When I was just beginning to study macrobiotics, I went up to Los Angeles for a weekend workshop with a macrobiotic teacher. One of the workshop students had brought her son, so the two of them could learn about macrobiotic cooking in hopes of addressing a health issue the boy had. On the last day of class, the student confided to the teacher that she and her family were having a hard time eating short-grain brown rice. They were from the Middle East, and they were used eating white basmati rice. The teacher insisted that they eat only short-grain brown rice; otherwise, the son's condition would not improve. The distraught look on the mother's face impacted me for a very long time. I knew enough about macrobiotics to understand why the teacher was recommending short-grain brown rice, but I felt that if the family couldn't eat brown rice, they wouldn't stick to the diet! There had to be other possibilities. Were there no other options to support this family's health crisis? Surely there was another way.

What happened to this family haunted me for many years, and I never forgot the disappointment on the mother's face. Years later when I was supporting friends and family in their switch to healthier meals, I came up with my "better than" theory. What if the teacher had felt compassion for the mother and offered a curving path to the desired goal, instead of a strict, straight, and narrow path? The teacher could have recommended combining organic white rice with brown basmati rice as a step in the transition to short-grain brown rice. Organic white basmati would be better than a commercial or a quick-cooking white rice. Then, after some time, the mother could mix brown basmati rice with short-grain brown rice and eventually replace all of the brown basmati rice with short-grain brown rice. For the teacher, this may have not been optimal, but for the family it was an option that would keep them following the program, which likely would have brought overall good health not just to the son but the whole family. And wouldn't that have been the healthiest option?

I've shared my "better than" theory with many, many people. Mothers, who are trying to improve their children's nutrition, use the "better than" approach to stay flexible on the way to their desired outcome—not as a control issue but as an effective life strategy. So how does the "better than" theory work? Start out by creating options that work for everyone. Then, very slowly, work up to where you want to be.

Let's use cereal, for example. I wasn't so fond of my kids eating sugary breakfast cereals, but they loved dry cereal in the morning, just like their friends. So we shopped for a not-so-sweet cereal (my choice) and mixed it with one that was sweeter (the kids' choice). I was happy, and the kids were happy. Drama-free change is possible. So remember the "better than" theory the next time you are at a party, out to dinner, or wanting a snack. What is a better option? There's always one item that's better than another, so use it to your advantage to stay on track.

a cup of tea

Tea has been a lifesaver for me, many more times than I can count. My love of tea blossomed when I was traveling with my mom in Europe during my summer in Sweden. Every afternoon, we would stop at a pastry shop and order a delicacy to share. My mom would order coffee, and because I hadn't developed a taste for that dark bold brew yet, I would order tea. I poured the rich half-and-half into my steamy hot cup of black tea and watched as it swirled around in my cup, creating clouds before blending in with the tea. I have fond memories of these moments shared with my mom, and thus, tea holds a special place in my heart. To this day, when I'm feeling I need a little comfort, I make a cup of Irish breakfast tea, add cream, and within moments I'm transported to a place where all is well. I feel emotionally full.

Not enough is said about the healing powers of tea. I have a high reverence for these tiny leaves because they played a huge role in my recovery and how I live my life currently. Early in my recovery, I realized that a binge was usually triggered because I was tired. One day, when I was exhausted, overwhelmed, and looking to food for energy, I had a revelation. I could press a "pause button" within myself by making a caffeinated cup of tea, sitting at the breakfast table, and taking deep, relaxing breaths. This ten-minute break, with caffeine now flowing through my body, lifted my spirits and allowed me to continue on with my afternoon activities with no need for any food, much less a binge. Tea time has practically become a daily ritual, and I look forward to the little break in my day to warm my soul and reawaken my energy.

When my first child, Joshua, was born, I needed support from other mothers who had insight into the many questions that were coming up for me about motherhood and parenting. So I started a tea group that met once a week, usually at my house. I would brew the tea, and the women would come with their children and bring a dish or dessert to share with the group. Over tea, we shared our wisdom and became a tight-knit group, often discussing topics way beyond motherhood and parenting. To this day, 25 years later, I still host morning gatherings with my very close girlfriends and serve cups of tea.

Chamomile tea is a favorite in my house. We drink this tea mostly in the evening and during the winter months. It makes for a great bedtime ritual and helps to prepare our bodies for sleep. My daughter asks for a cup of this special flower when she has an upset stomach or when she just wants to relax. For us, it definitely works its magic by calming and relaxing, so I always keep chamomile in my cupboard.

Years ago, I started making what I call "nutritional herbal tea" by brewing nettle leaves and milky oat tops. It's a powerhouse of herbal nutrition, and I always feel charged after I drink a cup. I brew my herbs to make a concentrate, strain out the leaves, and then I keep it in the fridge. This way, when I want a warm cup, I pour some of the concentrate into a cup and add boiling water to create the perfect temperature for drinking.

I make my nutritional herbal tea using mostly flowers and/or leaves. I boil water, turn off the heat, and let it sit for a couple of minutes. I place a 1/2 cup of nettles and a 1/2 cup of milky oat tops in a clean, glass quart jar. Then I pour the hot water over the leaves, cover the jar, and let the leaves sit anywhere from 30 minutes to 12 hours before straining out the herbs.

There are so many types of teas to explore. Find the ones that resonate with you, whether herbal or caffeinated. There are different ways to brew your teas, and in general, you can't go wrong. Brewing times for caffeinated teas range from 1 minute (green tea) to 5 minutes (black tea). Everyone likes tea at different strengths, so find a concentration that works for you. If your brew is too strong, add more hot water. If it's not strong enough, remember next time to add more leaves. There is no right or wrong way to enjoy your tea. Brewing yourself a cup is about taking a minute to make space for yourself in your busy life, to catch your breath, and to pause to enjoy the moment. For me, tea is one of the greatest blessings in my life.

food labels

Food labels should exist to inform, not confuse. Do not lose momentum by getting lost in the many issues surrounding food labeling. Here's a quick explanation of what I look for when buying food for my family.

As a mother to four children, I choose organic because I want the least amount of chemicals in their bodies. Their health is my responsibility, so I provide them with the cleanest food possible. Not only is it good for them but it's also good for the planet. To me, organic food also has more flavor and nutrients.

The jury is still out on genetically modified organisms (GMOs), but I purchase foods labeled with the Non-GMO Project Verified seal. The more I read, the more I find out about the negative effects that GMOs have, not only on humans but on all insects and animals. As I create our meals using as many organic and non-GMO ingredients as possible, I know I've done the best I can for all of Earth's inhabitants.

I also buy local and seasonal foods. When I say "local and seasonal," I'm referring to foods grown within a few hundred miles of where I live. To truck and transport foods from outside areas generally means higher prices because of gas and other resources needed to get the items from where they were grown to my local market. Also, buying local fruits and vegetables means my family and I are eating what's in season. Farmers' markets are great places to shop for local produce, meats, and dairy products.

Throughout the thirty-five years I've been involved with natural foods, I've learned a lot. I've gotten to where I am now through trial and error, reading and listening. With what I know, I have a basic idea of the foods I want to buy when I go shopping. But I also understand that everybody is in a different place. So if any of what I say rings true to you, embrace that which sounds right, and let go of what doesn't. I'm sharing what I have learned about food and invite you to change only what resonates with you.

You, too, are on your own journey and where you are is exactly where you are supposed to be. There is no need to stress over anything that doesn't feel right or feels overwhelming. Start with small steps.

dishes

Sometimes it's the small things that make all the difference in life. As we get closer to the recipe section of the book, I want to let you know how important color is to the whole process of cooking and eating, particularly in the appearance of meals. At one time, I wanted all my dishes and placemats to be the same color. However, shopping at a Japanese market in San Diego put a new twist on my thoughts about tableware. The variety of color I saw there stopped me in my tracks. Each dish color was more beautiful than the next. There were red, blue, green, and yellow dishes stacked together, not separated. All the colors together were so much richer than any one color. When I saw soup bowls, tea cups, and plates in assorted colors packed together in sets, I gave up my need for matching tableware. With various sets of colorful dishes in my bag and a variety of placemats at home, I knew my table would be full of color from now on. My family has had so much fun over the years choosing placemats, bowls, and plates to fit their moods. I enjoy serving food on colorful dishes as a feast for the eyes. No matter what mood I'm in, my spirit is always lifted when I see the vibrancy and richness in our beautiful table settings.

Paying attention to serving dishes also helps with portion control. Most American homes stock their cupboards with large dinner plates, oversized soup bowls, and voluminous drinking glasses. If you struggle with portion sizes, take a quick inventory of the dish sizes you use. Does a smaller portion of food on a large plate leave you feeling less satisfied? Do you take more food than you really need to be satisfied because you're eating out of a deep bowl? Think about this as you replace broken dishes, or go all out and purchase smaller, serving-size-appropriate tableware.

Years ago, I did an experiment with my children. I served chocolate pudding in two bowls of different sizes. In general, I like to use pudding bowls that hold about a 1/4 cup of dessert. This way, if they want more, I can give it to them because they started out with such a small amount. Most of the time, though, a small quantity satisfies them and they don't ask for more. On this particular day, I gave one of my boys his pudding in the smaller bowl, and my other son got his in a much larger bowl. They both got the same amount of pudding, but my son who got his in the larger bowl asked why he didn't get as much as his brother.

It is amazing what tricks the eyes can play on you. The smaller bowl, which was full, made it seem like one boy was getting more than his brother. On the other hand, a larger bowl makes it look like you are getting less, and you may not feel as satisfied regardless of the amount of food. For this reason, having smaller dishes that hold more reasonable portions can help the eye perceive that the quantity of food is enough to satisfy your hunger. Thus, if you want to control your portion sizes, try using smaller dishes.

During food preparation, the importance of color applies as well. As I do with my dishes, I always think about color when I put together my meal. Seeing bright yellow, green, red, or orange in a soup or salad attracts my eye and starts my digestive juices flowing. For example, if I make a black bean soup using only onion, garlic, potato, tomato, and cumin, the color of the soup might look *blah*. However, if I add some seasonal vegetables like corn, cilantro, carrot, or chopped red pepper, their colors give the soup an eye-catching look that makes me want grab a spoon and start eating. Even though both soups taste similar, the color in the second soup is more attractive to the eye, lifting my spirit. So when preparing your food, think about what colors you can add to brighten the presentation of your dish.

Several years ago, my niece came to live with us for six months to attend school. When she arrived, she confided to me that she wanted to lose weight while living in California. Here was an opportunity for me to test the concepts that I had come to learn over the years about eating issues. I explained my ideas, gave her some instruction, and with my support, she started on her journey of changing her relationship with food.

Basically, she ate three meals a day plus snacks in between if she wanted them. There were no limits on her food choices. The biggest difference was that the food she ate at our home was served on small, Japanese-style dishes. She mentioned to me that the smaller dishes did help her to eat less. She also learned to ask herself, after her first serving of food, if she was really hungry enough to take a second helping. As a result, when she would go out to eat, she had a good idea of healthy portion sizes.

Over a few months, she became more aware of hunger and fullness. Occasionally, she'd want more food at dinner, but she knew that if she wanted a cup of chamomile tea and a dessert later while doing her homework, it was better to forego a second helping at dinner. After six months, she went back home weighing fifty pounds less than when she arrived! No dieting, no calorie counting, no bad or good foods, no hunger, no endless exercising, and no craziness. She just listened to her body, and it told her what it needed. Nothing more, nothing less.

We also talked about weighing herself less frequently. I didn't want the numbers on the scale to influence how she felt about herself. Weighing herself only a couple of times a month helped her stay in touch with her body and focus on her portion sizes. She gained confidence in herself and knew that she could monitor the quantity of food she ate to keep herself healthy, both physically and mentally. I was so proud of her and her accomplishments. Her results also confirmed my thoughts on conscious eating. If I could do it and she could do it, others could, too. This new sense of balance became a part of her everyday life. Who wouldn't want that?

portion sizes

You may notice, when you read my recipes, I don't mention the number of servings a recipe makes. This is intentional. What our bodies require differs with each day and each meal. By omitting suggested servings, I'm inviting you to decide how much you wish to eat of any food. For example, if I've had a grain dish for breakfast, I may choose, at dinner, to skip the grain and have two bowls of soup instead. I give myself permission to decide what my body is asking for by checking in regularly and going with what my instincts tell me.

Each of my family members has a different appetite. My husband doesn't consume much food during the day, so in general, he eats most of his food at dinner. My daughter, on the other hand, chooses smaller quantities because she eats three meals a day. When my son, Noah, was a cross-country runner, he needed more food and more calories. I understand that, as individual requirements vary, so do portion sizes. Each of us needs to consume enough fuel to perform our daily activities, and we know best what we need.

The same guidelines apply for snacks and sweets. When I bake cookies, I change the size according to how I'm feeling that day. If the cookies are bigger, I may be satisfied with one. If I have made them much smaller, I might enjoy three. This is another way I have become free: there is no right or wrong serving size. I encourage you to decide, meal by meal, what the best serving size is for yourself. Your body knows what it needs, and it will tell you, if you listen to its quiet voice.

chewing

So far, I've shared the importance of having appropriate dish sizes, colorful food presentation, and present-moment awareness while eating. Now let's talk about chewing. Chewing is another tool that can help you eat less. I first learned the art of chewing when I studied macrobiotics, and it has become one of my best habits. Why is it a good habit? Our teeth are designed to crush food and mix it with saliva, which is the first stage of digestion. The more you chew your food, the easier it is on your digestive system. Your stomach doesn't have to work as hard to break down the food, and well-chewed food helps the body extract and absorb nutrients. But this is not the only reason to chew well. Focusing on chewing helps to keep you present and in the moment. You become more aware of when you are satisfied or feeling full. When I eat fast and chew less, my brain doesn't have time to catch up to the food I'm consuming. By the time my stomach and brain get their communication straight, I've usually eaten a lot more food than I expected.

When I was first learning to chew well, I would practice by taking a spoonful of rice and counting how many times I could chew it before feeling the need to swallow. I wasn't very successful in the beginning, but with each mouthful, I would chew a little bit longer than the time before. Slowly but surely, I got the hang of it, and sometimes I'd catch myself chewing nearly fifty times. Yes, that is a lot of chewing, and as you might guess, different types of food take different amounts of time to chew completely. For me, bread and grain take the most amount of chewing, while cooked vegetables and fruit require less. So, are you up for giving chewing a try? As you take each bite and begin counting, notice all of the flavors and textures your taste buds are sensing. How does your body feel? It may seem strange at first, but it won't be long before you automatically count chews each time you eat, ultimately keeping you present. As with many things, it will take practice and patience to learn this art, but from experience, I will tell you, it's well worth it.

other choices

You will notice that the recipes in this book are vegetarian. Most of my life I have been a vegetarian; avoiding meat works for me. As a child, when given a choice, I mostly chose vegetarian options. So when I made the conscious decision to become vegetarian, it came very easily to me. In my experience, children usually know what's best for their bodies and what their nutritional needs are, if given healthy options. Some of my children eat poultry, and I have always allowed them to make this decision for themselves. Many animals raised for food are treated with hormones and antibiotics, which affects the quality of meat and milk products. I do my best to avoid hormone-laden animal products by buying the best-quality meat and dairy products I can find for my children.

Over the years, I've instilled in my children one lesson I learned many years ago: "If you are going to buy meat or dairy, buy the best quality. If it's too expensive, buy less and eat less." I do eat eggs and some dairy products but not a lot. Once again, this is just my preference. For me, a little goes a long way, and I don't deny myself the pleasure of cream, cheese, butter, and ice cream. When I eat dairy, I choose organic and raw if available. Goat's milk and its cheeses are my first choice because I just love the flavor. Keep in mind that my choices around meat and dairy have nothing to do with denying myself or my children anything. The focus is on keeping ourselves healthy and happy. Think about food in these terms, and a peaceful and healthy relationship with food will follow.

Always, always remember that this is your life. There is no judge or jury here, no one who has an expectation of what your journey should look like. Allow your healing to unfold according to what works for you. The recipes I share here are just ideas and suggestions that have worked well for me. My hope is that my journey will provide some inspiration for you on your journey.

Your process will be your own. If life is hectic, and you don't have time to cook beans or grains, there are plenty of canned beans or quick-cooking grains available to you. If you are unable to get the vegetables that are in my recipes, use the ones that you find in your local market. You can use frozen vegetables for your soups and dried herbs instead of fresh, too! Remember, you can add any type of meat or dairy to many of the dishes as well. If you can't find organic or some other food specified in a recipe, make it with what you can find. What sounds good to you? What's within reach?

This dance isn't about rules and being rigid. It is about adapting and changing, flowing with life. Each of us has different financial obligations and time constraints, so your dance in the kitchen must fit your life. And, when you are ready, try something new, and see how it works for you.

This is the beginning of your journey—a time of transformation and taking care of yourself. It's the beginning of a new and healthy relationship with food. So go ahead, take that first step. In no time, you will be dancing in your kitchen, and the richness and beauty of what that creates will nourish not just your body but also your soul!

And that secret I mentioned earlier? My Zen practice. I had to give up the need for control to find the peace and contentment I was trying to provide for myself with control. In the process of letting go, I found what I needed. I found out that life isn't about the "shoulds" and "shouldn'ts" I had created for myself. It's about balance. My life had been made up of so many rules to keep myself safe that I'd become deathly afraid of breaking any of them. It wasn't until I was able to let go of the need for control and all of my rigid, inflexible rules that I was able to recover completely.

Once I set aside my armor, with no rules to follow, I freed myself. I was free to try out new ideas, and if they didn't work, I tried something else. Control shifted to present-moment awareness, and I connected my emotional, physical, and mental parts into a whole me. I recognized that life really is about the journey, not the arrival. Our lives are worth celebrating every day, and what better way to celebrate than by cooking good food and sharing it with family and friends? I have created a beautiful dance in my kitchen, and it is a joyous dance.

After all is said and done, what would I like you to walk away with after reading the story of my journey? I'd love for you to feel a sense of calm. Take a breath. I'd like you to believe that you can do anything, even though it may take time and hard work. My father-in-law, who was born in Baghdad, used to always say, "All good things come to those with wait and faith." Every word of this book was written with patience and faith. I hope that my story and my recipes inspire you to start dancing down the road toward a peaceful relationship with food, leaving behind anything that doesn't serve you. Can you hear the music? Let's start dancing.

Part 2: Recipes

I had a huge revelation putting my favorite recipes together for this book. I had always wondered why some recipes in cookbooks and magazines specified name brands in the ingredients list. I think I now know why. As I was testing my recipe for Best Balls Ever!, making sure it was bulletproof for the book, I ran out of my usual honey. *No worries*, I thought, *I've got many other honeys to choose from*. I went on to prepare the balls with a different honey, but once all the ingredients were together and I was ready to roll them into balls, the dough was too wet. *Yikes!* I thought. *What happened?* Well, my usual honey is thicker than the one I substituted. The thinner honey created a different consistency in the batter. As a troubleshooting measure, I added more rice bran solubles, and that fixed the problem. Being aware of the uniqueness of each type of ingredient will make your experience with the following recipes even more successful, yummy, and enjoyable.

Keep in mind that the products you use to make the recipes will most likely be different than the ones I use because there are so many varieties and brands out there. So be aware that each type and brand of flour, peanut butter, dry beans, salt, etcetera will have a slightly different flavor, consistency, and reaction during baking or cooking. For example, when you follow a cookie recipe, add the flour slowly, so you can see how much is needed to get the desired dough texture. Also, your preference for saltiness may be different than mine, so amounts used should reflect your taste, not mine. When you are making soup, add salt slowly, so you can see how much is necessary. This way, you can adjust the recipes to your taste and to the brands you use for cooking and baking.

This being said, many of my recipes list just the basic ingredients. For example, a cookie recipe will call for "flour." Even though I use a gluten-free variety, you can use any kind. Do you want to use white flour or whole wheat flour instead of gluten free? It's up to you. Just watch for the right consistency, and adjust accordingly. Similarly, when I use the word "salt" in my recipes, know that I'm using either sea salt or a Himalayan variety, but you have the option of using any type.

Now, I'd like to invite you into my kitchen to see what I prepare for my family and the type of food that has helped me along my road to recovery. Each recipe you are about to read has been made multiple times and with different twists. These recipes have been taking care of me and those dearest to me for many years. I am so blessed to have the opportunity to share them with you now.

soups

clear broth

clear broth

I just love this broth! It is light but also full of goodness for your body. I like to call it "liquid gold." It's a beautiful sight to behold when the refrigerator door is opened, and there, sitting on the shelf, gleaming in clear glass jars, Clear Broth awaits its use in a recipe. Clear Broth can be used as an alternative to a cup of tea in the afternoon—warm and nurturing. It is so delicious warmed up with a pinch of sea salt. Although I use this broth mostly for Miso Soup (page 27), it can be used in any soup or grain recipe. Use Clear Broth instead of water for making savory rice, preparing soup, or cooking beans. It is liquid gold, for sure. Feel free to double the recipe so that you have more broth to use in other dishes over the course of the week. I sometimes make my broth concentrated, so I don't need to use as much.

3 quarts water	2 dried shiitake mushrooms, sliced (soaked and stems removed)
2- to 3-inch piece kombu seaweed	
2 tablespoons dried burdock root or one fresh root, diced (cleaned with a vegetable brush)	Vegetable trimmings you have saved over the week (See examples below.)
1 yellow onion, diced	

Place all of the ingredients, except for the vegetable trimmings, in a large pot. Bring to a boil without the lid. Once boiling, reduce the heat and allow the mixture to simmer for 20 minutes.

After 20 minutes, add the vegetable trimmings. Not sure what that means? Many times when prepping vegetables, you may find parts that are wilted, brown, or just not really fresh. Save these parts by collecting them in a plastic bag and storing the bag in your refrigerator. When you are ready to make your broth, wash the trimmings, and prepare them to be added to the pot. Sometimes, if the core of a cauliflower or cabbage has been in the fridge for several days, the ends may be dry or discolored. With my knife, I remove a thin layer where needed before I do my chopping.

If you are just getting started on adding the richness of vegetables to your life and don't have trimmings, the broth can be made with just the onion and kombu. Remember, it's not about being perfect; it's about making the best choice you can at any given time. Make a wonderful broth however you choose. If you can get organic ingredients, do it! They're a treasure to savor. But if not, work with what you have. Don't let anything stop you from feeding yourself well. As time goes on, and you prepare more meals at home, you may find that you have plenty of trimmings for your broth, including these:

Core of a cauliflower, cut into quarters and then sliced	Corn cobs, kernels removed
Core of a cabbage, sliced	Outer leaves of a leek, washed and sliced
Outer leaves of a cauliflower or cabbage, cubed or sliced	Carrot sticks leftover from lunches or snacks

During cold and flu season, you can add a few sticks of dried Astragalus to help boost immunity. Once the vegetable trimmings are placed in the pot, stir them into the liquid and simmer for another 20 minutes. Turn off the heat and strain out the vegetables. Use a colander or metal strainer placed in a large, non-plastic bowl, or use whatever you have in your kitchen. Pour the broth through the strainer into the bowl, lifting the strainer out and placing it back into your pot to finish draining. Using a metal or glass measuring cup—a coffee cup works well, too—pour your broth into clean glass jars (e.g., Mason jars, peanut butter jars, or pasta jars). Let the liquid cool before placing the lids on your jars. I find covering the jars with sushi mats (bamboo mats) works well for cooling food items. They allow the heat to escape during cooling while preventing anything from getting in. Store the broth in the refrigerator for up to one week.

miso soup

miso soup

During the cool months of spring, autumn, and winter, you will usually find bowls of Miso Soup at our breakfast table. Grounding and warming, Miso Soup gets the body's engine running and ready to take on the day.

There are many types of miso paste available in health food stores, Asian markets, or online. I feel it is important to find a miso that is unpasteurized, organic, and a non-GMO variety. But as always, work with what you can find. I like to use the lighter chickpea miso for my family because it has a very gentle flavor, which my kids love. During the winter months a stronger miso can be used, while a warm summer calls for a lighter one. The rule of thumb is the longer the miso has been aged, the stronger the flavor. Depending on the brand and how long the miso has been aged, one type of miso may be saltier than another. In this recipe, I recommend about 1 teaspoon of miso paste per person, but you can add more or less depending on how salty you prefer your soup. When I buy a new brand or variety of miso paste, I always taste my soup before serving to make sure it has the flavor I desire. If it doesn't have enough flavor, I add more miso to the soup. If your soup is too strong or salty, you can add more water or broth.

> 3/4 cup Clear Broth (page 25)
> 1/2 teaspoon wakame seaweed
> 1 teaspoon miso paste

I use an instant wakame because it is quick and easy. If you use wakame that is still on the stem, it will need to be soaked first. Be aware that a small amount goes a long way. This seaweed expands quite a bit when it is placed in water. After the seaweed is soft, remove leaves from the stem, slice them thin, and place the leaves into the pot with the Clear Broth. I recommend that you start off using a small amount of wakame and gradually add more as you get accustomed to the flavor.

Bring the broth with the wakame up to a simmer. While the broth is heating, mix 1 teaspoon of miso paste per person in a dish with a small amount of water. (You can also take some of the warm broth from the pot and add it to the miso paste.) Once the broth is simmering and the miso paste is made, turn the heat to low. At this point, add your miso paste and stir. Quail eggs are a wonderful addition to Miso Soup. If you can find them in a market near you, try them in this soup. They are delicious. If you're using quail eggs, this is a good time to put them in. I leave the eggs in the hot broth for about 2 minutes to cook and then scoop them out and place them in individual bowls. Now turn off the heat under the pot and ladle the soup into the bowls. Garnish with some chopped green onion, parsley, or cilantro. What a wonderful way to start a day, warm an afternoon, or begin a dinner. Miso Soup never fails to leave my family feeling loved and nurtured.

french onion soup

french onion soup

My oldest son, Joshua, loves this soup! It's pretty simple, yet very delicious. I believe that you'll love this vegetarian version, and it'll become a favorite.

> **3 to 4 onions, cut in half then very thinly sliced (the thinner, the better)**
> **2 tablespoons olive oil**
> **Pinch of sea salt**
> **4 cups Clear Broth (page 25)**
> **Soy sauce to taste**
> **Grated cheese, breadcrumbs, or parsley for garnish**

In a preheated pot, combine the onions and olive oil. Add salt to bring out the sweetness, and sauté on medium heat for 5 to 10 minutes, stirring regularly. Place a lid on the pot, reduce the heat to low, and set a flame tamer under the pot. A flame tamer is a metal heat diffuser that sits between the bottom of a pot and the burner. It keeps the heat under the pot even and low, allowing the onions to cook on the lowest heat possible without scorching. Let the onions cook this way for at least 3 hours; the longer they cook, the sweeter they will become.

After the onions have cooked, remove the flame tamer from under the pot. Pour the Clear Broth into the pot, and turn up the heat to bring the soup to just below a boil. Add soy sauce to taste. It may take a couple of tablespoons or so to get the desired flavor, depending on the brand you use. Remember to taste the soup as you add the soy sauce to get your desired saltiness. Ladle the soup into bowls and garnish as desired.

beans and bean soups

Bean soups are one of my favorite meals. I say "meal" because I am usually satisfied with a large bowl of soup, and it meets many of my nutritional criteria as well. So many vegetables can be put into soup, and together with the beans, this becomes a heartwarming dish. My youngest son, Noah, once asked me why we always have soup. "Simple," I told him. "I want you to eat a lot of vegetables." My kids have never been fond of raw salad, so for me, soup was the easiest and best way to get them to have a variety of vegetables.

I'm going to share a few of my favorite bean soup recipes, which you can always use to create your own version. Take a moment before you make your soup, and think about the color, taste, and texture you are looking for in what you are about to create. Remember that any amount of vegetable you use will be perfect; the more, the merrier. Imagine how nutritious your soup will become.

First, I decide on which vegetables and how much of each one I want to use in my soup. Some days, I use more greens because I haven't had the amount of greens I feel I need for that particular day. On other days, I may be craving a sweeter soup, so I add more carrot, corn, or kabocha squash. I recommend starting light on seasoning and adding more as needed. It's always easier to add more salt and herbs after you've sampled your soup than to remove it later by adding more liquid. Less is always best; start off in small increments, and add to taste. It may be a good idea to jot down the variations you try and note your favorites. This way, going back and recreating your "dance" will be easy.

A rule of thumb for making soup is this: Harder vegetables or vegetables prepped into larger pieces should be added to your soup first. Lighter or smaller-sized ones should be added later, with the exception of onion. Onion becomes sweeter the longer it is cooked, so it goes into the pot first. Using your intuition, just think about what makes sense, and then go for it.

For example, which takes more time to cook: spinach or carrots? Carrots do, so they would go into your pot earlier in the process than the spinach. How about cauliflower or broccoli? A tougher question, yes? They are both flowerets, but when you look at them, broccoli flowerets are more open and softer than cauliflower flowerets. If you were putting them together in a dish, the cauliflower would be added first and the broccoli just a bit later. Don't worry if you don't know which cooks faster. Just figure that denser vegetables take more time. The worst that can happen is some vegetables may become softer than you planned, but over time, you will get a sense of the order and timing of placing the vegetables into the pot—it's all good.

Something else to keep in mind, and similar to what I mentioned about salt and flour, is this: not all vegetables are created equal. Depending on how they're grown, some vegetables contain more or less water than others of the same variety, leading to a longer or shorter cooking time.

Because of this, I taste the vegetables in my soups as they are cooking to see where they are in the cooking process. Tasting as you go is an important step in the cooking dance, and it ensures a finished dish that you will be excited to serve and eat.

beans

On any given day, you can open my refrigerator and find a quart or two of cooked beans inside, side by side with my jars of liquid gold broth. I am a big fan of these little gems and their ability to make delicious soups and salads. There are endless ways to use them to enhance the flavor of any dish. They are so good for you! Beans come in all different colors, sizes, and shapes, and if they are not a staple in your pantry now, I hope they will be soon. Most countries have a bean that is common to their area, and lucky for us, we can buy many of them here in the United States. Of course, my family has some favorites, but that doesn't stop me from bringing in new varieties to try. Who knows? One may become a new favorite. Our local farmers' market has freshly dried beans of all varieties, mostly ones you don't see in grocery stores. So I buy colorful ones, big ones, and small ones to test out on my family because it's always good to change ingredients a bit whenever I can.

Busy lives can make it difficult to make meals at home from scratch, especially if recipes contain beans, which can take time to prepare. What works best for me is to make beans in advance so that I can come home and put together a meal in a short amount of time. I find a day of the week when I will be home for a few hours, and I make that my bean cooking day. Evenings can also be a good time to cook beans for the next day or for later in the week. If I have a busy week coming up, I may prepare a few different types of beans to store in my fridge. They will be there when I get home, ready to become a part of a quick and delicious meal.

First, I decide on the types of beans I want to prepare and how much of each type I want to have on hand. Then, I measure out each type into a separate bowl and sort through them for stones. This can be done easily by spreading out a small batch of beans onto a plate and picking through them.

Once the stones have been removed, place the beans into a bowl or pot for soaking. Cover the beans with filtered water, and let them soak for 8 to 12 hours, depending on your schedule. Beans can triple in size while soaking, so be sure to add enough water. I usually cook my beans in the morning or evening, so I soak them either the night before, for morning cooking, or in the morning, for evening cooking. After the beans have soaked, I wash and rinse them many times. It is not mandatory to soak beans, but it does shorten the cooking time and can reduce or eliminate the gas experienced by some people.

Place the clean beans into a pot and cover them with water, about two inches above the beans. Put the pot on top of a burner and bring it to a boil. Most beans produce white foam that can be easily skimmed off and discarded. This foam can produce gas, so it is good to remove it. Continue to simmer the beans uncovered for 10 minutes or so, removing any foam that bubbles to the top. After 10 minutes, place a 1-inch piece of kombu seaweed per cup of dry beans into the pot and cover. Turn the heat to low and allow the beans to cook until they are soft. The type, size, and age of the beans determine the length of cooking time required. Taste the beans throughout the cooking process, and once they are soft, stir in approximately 1/2 teaspoon of good-quality salt per cup of dry beans. Simmer for 10 more minutes to allow the salt to penetrate the beans. If you add salt to your beans at the beginning of cooking, it can prevent them from softening.

For example, if are you are preparing 2 cups of dry beans, you would use a 2-inch piece of kombu and 1 teaspoon of salt for seasoning. Remember, each type of salt has a different degree of salinity, so start with smaller amounts, adding more as needed. I recommend you taste your beans for flavor as they are salted and before they are finished.

pinto bean soup

pinto bean soup

Living in Southern California near the Mexican border, we have some of the best Mexican restaurants in the country, and pinto beans are a staple. I don't recall ever having pinto beans while I was growing up in northern Wisconsin, but once I moved to San Diego, these "local" beans became my bean of choice.

Pinto beans are a medium-sized bean with a light brown color. They are easy to prepare and have a mild flavor. They are one type of bean that I make on a weekly basis, and one that is loved by all of my family. I make a large pot of beans, so I have enough to last for several days of making delicious soups, salads, and a signature dish of mine, Mexican Lasagna (page 73). Without further ado, here is the recipe for my Pinto Bean Soup!

1 tablespoon olive oil
1 cup onion, diced (large or small pieces)
6 small, fresh shiitake mushrooms
3 to 4 cups water
1/2 teaspoon sea salt (or to taste)
4 medium carrots, sliced in 1/4-inch rounds
3 to 4 cups baby spinach, washed, stems removed, and chopped

2 teaspoons freshly grated turmeric or 1/4 to 1/2 teaspoon dried turmeric
1 medium garlic clove, minced
2 cups cooked pinto beans (See cooking instructions on page 33.)
Cilantro leaves

Most of my soups contain onion. No matter what bean or vegetable I'm using, I start with onion because when it is sautéed in oil with a pinch of salt, it becomes very sweet. I prefer to use olive oil to sauté my onions, but you can use butter, coconut oil, sesame oil, or whatever oil you have on hand.

I tend to avoid oils like corn, soy, or canola, many of which are grown with GMOs. I also limit the amount of oils containing omega-6 fatty acids. Both of these choices came out of doing a lot of research, and I encourage you to read up on oils and come to a conclusion that is best suited for you. As always, don't let all of the information and options deter you from making a yummy pot of soup. Just make the best choice you can, and enjoy the savory warmth of your creation.

In a warm, medium-sized pot, combine the olive oil and onion, sautéing until translucent. Add the mushrooms and allow them cook for a few minutes. Next add the water and salt, bringing the soup to a soft boil. Reduce the heat and add the carrots. When the carrots are about 50 percent cooked, add the spinach, turmeric, garlic, and pinto beans. Over medium heat, again bring the soup to just below a boil. Be sure that the carrots are the right tenderness for you and that the spinach has wilted and turned a bright green. At this point, taste your soup, and adjust the flavor by adding more salt or turmeric. Turn off the heat.

Garnish your bowls of soup with cilantro, or (if you are a lover of this green like I am) stir a handful of the leaves into the pot before serving. I generally top my soup with several slices of avocado. I love the flavor and healthy fat that it offers. Once in a while, I sprinkle some grated goat cheese on top as a garnish. Yum!

split pea soup

split pea soup

As a child I remember trying split pea soup at a restaurant one time. To be honest, one bite was all I needed to decide that it was not a soup for me. I don't know if it was the ham, saltiness, or what, but I was hesitant to ever try the soup again. To my surprise, years later I braved a small spoonful at a macrobiotic restaurant, and fell in love! This soup is one that Jimbo really likes, and so it has become one of the soups I enjoy preparing during the winter months, knowing that my husband loves it.

Split peas, once cooked, are creamy and delicious. In general, you will find yellow and green varieties, and for this recipe, you can use either. I love the green color, so I usually choose this one for my soups. The cooking time for split peas is reduced quite a bit if the peas are soaked first. Although some cookbooks don't recommend soaking, I always do.

2 cups dry, green split peas, soaked 6 to 8 hours

2-inch piece kombu seaweed

1 teaspoon sea salt (or to taste)

1 medium onion, diced or thinly sliced into half-moon shapes

1 tablespoon olive oil

6 fresh shiitake mushrooms

2 burdock roots (cleaned with a vegetable brush), sliced in half lengthwise and then julienned

3 cups water

2 medium potatoes, peeled and cubed

4 carrots, sliced

1/4 teaspoon (or to taste) sea salt

1 bunch spinach, washed and torn into small pieces

1 garlic clove, minced

Dash of nutmeg (optional)

Wash and rinse the soaked split peas well. Place the clean peas into a pot, and cover them with water by two inches. Bring the water to a boil. Foam will rise to the surface as the peas come to a boil. Skim off the foam and discard. Allow the peas to simmer for a few minutes, and continue to remove the foam. When no more foam is being produced, add the kombu, and then cover the pot with a lid. Check the peas regularly, to be sure there is enough water, and give them a stir. As split peas cook, they become creamy and sink to the bottom of the pot, so stir them often. If you prefer a thick soup, allow the peas to cook with the least amount of water possible. Remember, as split peas cool, they thicken. Once the peas are soft and creamy, add 1 teaspoon of salt or to taste, and set them aside. Allow them to sit until the next steps are completed.

Heat a separate pot, and when the pot is warm, add the onion and olive oil, sautéing until the onion is translucent. Next add the mushrooms and burdock roots, mixing them well into the onion. Add 1 cup of water and a 1/4 teaspoon salt, and allow these ingredients to simmer for 10 minutes. (The burdock roots need this cooking time to soften.) Now add 2 more cups of water, along with the potatoes. Bring the ingredients back up to a simmer, and let the potatoes cook for about 5 minutes before adding the carrots. Then, just before the carrots are tender, add the spinach and garlic to the pot along with the cooked split peas. Mix everything together, making sure to bring the vegetables from the bottom of the pot up to the top. Let everything cook together until the spinach wilts. Now your delicious Split Pea Soup is ready to be served. Don't forget to adjust the flavor!

It may seem odd, but years ago I heard that adding a dash of nutmeg to Split Pea Soup makes it more delicious. Try it sometime and see if you like it; I definitely do.

black bean soup

black bean soup

When I was a senior in high school, my parents took me and my siblings to Florida for spring break. We ate at a local Cuban restaurant where we had black beans for the first time. They tasted fabulous and inspired me to create another bean recipe to have under my belt.

Petite black beans are also quite mild, and they pair well with many different vegetable combinations. This is my favorite Black Bean Soup! In the summertime, I make a mean Black Bean Salad (page 59) that makes me feel like I'm in the Caribbean.

1 onion, diced
1 tablespoon olive oil
1 large tomato, cubed
2 cups water
1 cup corn (or more if you'd like), fresh or frozen
3 cups cooked black beans (See cooking instructions on page 33.)
1 bunch cilantro leaves
1 large garlic clove
1/4 teaspoon cumin
Sea salt to taste

In a preheated pot, sauté the onion and oil. When the onion is translucent, stir in the tomato and a pinch of salt, and cook for 5 minutes. Add 2 cups of water to the pot, and bring to a boil. Then add the corn. After a few minutes of cooking, add the cooked black beans, bringing them up to a simmer. Once the soup is simmering, stir in the cilantro, garlic, and cumin. Taste the soup, and adjust the flavor. You can top the soup with avocado, cheese, sour cream, green onion, or more cilantro. Whatever garnish you choose, enjoy this beautiful combination of Caribbean flavors.

red lentil soup

red lentil soup

There are days when I get home in the afternoon and realize that I forgot to soak beans for dinner. I check the fridge and there are no shining glass jars filled with my favorite gems, and I think, What am I going to do? No worries, I have red lentils. Red lentils are tiny orange legumes that really need no soaking. If I do choose to soak them, it's just for 1 hour. I recommend keeping them on hand for those emergencies when life happens, and you need something tasty that can be put together quickly.

Just as the recipe for the Split Pea Soup (page 37) has two pots going at the same time, so does this one. In one pot, cook the red lentils, and by the time the vegetables are prepped and cooked in a separate pot, the lentils will be finished and ready to marry with the vegetables to become this amazing soup.

  2 cups red lentils
  5 cups water or Clear Broth (page 25)
  1-inch piece kombu seaweed
  1 onion, diced
  1 tablespoon olive oil
  3 cups water
  1/2 teaspoon curry powder (or to taste)
  2 to 3 carrots, washed and diced into 1/2-inch cubes
  Cauliflower (as much as you want), separated into small flowerets of the same size
  1 cup peas, fresh or frozen
  1 garlic clove, minced
  1-1/2 teaspoons sea salt
  Cilantro leaves

Wash the red lentils several times, and then drain. Combine the lentils and water or broth in a pot. Bring to a boil, and then reduce the heat to a simmer. Skim off and discard any foam. Add kombu, and place a lid on the pot. Allow the lentils to cook for 30 to 45 minutes, adding more water if necessary. When the lentils are soft and creamy, add 1 teaspoon salt, and simmer for a few minutes more.

While the lentils are simmering, heat a second pot. Place the onion and olive oil in the pot and sauté until the onions are translucent. Next add 3 cups of water, curry powder, and a 1/2 teaspoon salt. Bring the water to a boil and add the carrots. After a minute, add the cauliflower. Allow these vegetables to simmer for a couple of minutes, and then add peas and garlic to the medley. After a few more minutes, add the cooked lentils to the vegetables and mix together gently. Add the cilantro and taste your soup, adjusting the flavor if needed. You might just find that you have a new favorite in this no-prep soup.

creamy potato leek soup

creamy potato leek soup

The men in my life love potatoes—potato anything—so this soup is for them. Jimbo prefers it thick, and it is another one of his favorites. Our horse trainer, Diana, loves this soup because it brings her to that peaceful place. Last fall, when she was going to have surgery, I told her that I would make some food for her. While I was listing some dishes I could make, she asked if I would make my Creamy Potato Leek Soup. Years before Diana became our trainer, she babysat our boys regularly and enjoyed this soup at our house on many occasions.

I love the way the leeks are hidden among the potatoes, adding some extra nutrients, and how the browned garlic sends your taste buds into a happy dance. So for Diana and all you potato lovers, this recipe is for you!

6 medium to large potatoes, peeled and diced into 1-inch cubes	**3 to 4 leeks (See recipe for preparation.)**
1/2 teaspoon sea salt (or to taste)	**4 or more garlic cloves, thinly sliced**
Pinch of freshly cracked pepper	**1 tablespoon olive oil**

With potatoes, it is important is to have cubes that are similar in size, so that they cook evenly. Place the potatoes, salt, and pepper into a pot, covering everything with water. Bring the water to a boil, reduce the heat to low, and place a lid ajar on the pot.

Leeks can have a little or a lot of dirt in between their leaves. Try to purchase leeks that have long, white trunks and smaller amounts of green on the top. They are easier to clean. Start by removing any outer leaves that are damaged, wilted, or tough, one at a time, until you get to the more tender leaves. These tender leaves may be three to four layers under the outer one, so save the removed layers for Clear Broth (page 25). Trim off any roots sparingly to preserve as much of the leek as possible. From the top of the leek, trim away any brown or jagged edges. On the outermost layer of the leek, look from the top down to see where the green color is split. Where it becomes solid green, separate the green top from the white bottom with a knife.

Take the green segment, open each layer, and rinse out any dirt that may be inside. Continue this process until the layers are free of dirt. The inner green section is more tender, so once again, save the tough outer or wilted layers in a bag in the refrigerator for Clear Broth. Slice the clean leeks into approximately 1-inch rounds.

When the potatoes just start to become tender, place the leeks on top and close the lid. Allow the soup to simmer until the leeks are tender. At this point, taste the broth and adjust the salt to your liking, letting the broth simmer a few more minutes. Turn off the heat. With a ladle or measuring cup, move the leeks to one side of the pot, and go underneath them to remove some potatoes with broth. Place the potatoes and broth into a blender. To create a very creamy soup, I blend about half of the potatoes. You can blend the whole batch or none of it. What's your mood, and what texture are you looking for? Once the potatoes are blended, pour them back into the pot, and mix the leeks back into the soup. You are almost done.

In a preheated skillet, place the sliced garlic in the olive oil, and sauté until the garlic becomes golden brown. (I let it brown slowly over low heat.) The garlic will become crispy, which I love. I place the garlic on top of the soup and serve. This allows Jimbo and the kids to serve themselves as much garlic as they choose. Another other option is to stir the garlic into the soup; however you choose, it will be scrumptious.

great northern bean soup

great northern bean soup

When Jimbo and I were first married, one of our stomping grounds was an Italian restaurant not too far from our home. I've never been a big pasta person, but this place made a fabulous pasta fagioli. The white beans, pasta, and tomato were delicious! Because I love the challenge of re-creating great-tasting food from restaurants, I was inspired to duplicate this soup at home. I am happy to say that I was successful! Over the years, it has deliciously mutated to this recipe. It reminds me of my Soul Soup (page 119) but with an Italian flair. Make some garlic bread to dip into this soup, and you just might feel like you are in Italia!

1 onion, diced

1 teaspoon to 1 tablespoon olive oil

3 cups water

1/2 teaspoon sea salt

2 tablespoons tomato paste

3 to 4 medium carrots, sliced into 1/2-inch rounds

3 cups cabbage, shredded

Fresh basil, sliced down the center and then thinly sliced (dried works well, too)

1 to 2 garlic cloves, minced

2 to 3 cups cooked great northern beans (See cooking instructions on page 33.)

Okay, you guessed it: sauté the onion in the olive oil. When the onions are translucent, add the water, salt, and tomato paste to the pot. Bring the contents to a boil, and then add the carrots. Simmer a few minutes, and then add the cabbage. When the carrots are just about tender, add the fresh basil and garlic. Add the cooked great northern beans and mix thoroughly. Adjust the salt and herbs at this time. Next, scoop some into a bowl and savor! *Buon appetito!*

sweet chickpea soup

sweet chickpea soup

Some days I'm in the mood for sweets but not the cookie or cake type. This soup "takes the cake" and nutritiously diminishes any craving for dessert. I have to say, it really is the most delicious soup ever. Some people enjoy dessert after dinner, but if you wish to avoid sugary desserts, then this is the soup for you. Grab your favorite bowl and sip slowly, mmm. In the fall when sweet winter squashes are plentiful and corn is ripe on the cob, they find their way into one of my pots, where they dance with beans and carrots. Your taste buds will desire nothing else!

    1 onion, halved and very thinly sliced
    1 teaspoon to 1 tablespoon olive oil
    2 cups kabocha, butternut, or buttercup squash, cubed (skin and seeds removed)
    3 cups water
    1/2 teaspoon curry powder
    1/2 teaspoon sea salt
    2 medium carrots, cut in half lengthwise and sliced into 1/2-inch half moons
    1 cup corn, fresh or frozen
    3 cups spinach or kale leaves, cut into 2-inch pieces (washed and kale stems removed)
    3 cups cooked chickpeas (See cooking instructions on page 33.)
    Cilantro leaves, green onion, or parsley for garnish

In a preheated pot, combine the onion with olive oil. Sauté the onion until it is translucent. Next add the squash, and sauté for 5 minutes. Add the water, curry powder, and salt, bringing the contents to a boil. Simmer for a few minutes until the squash begins to soften. Now add the carrots, and cook for a few minutes before adding the corn. When the carrots are tender, add the spinach. After a few minutes, when the spinach begins to wilt, add the cooked chickpeas. Mix them into the vegetables, and bring the soup to just under a boil. Taste your creation, and adjust the flavors. Spoon into bowls and garnish with chopped cilantro, green onion, parsley, or any other item that comes to mind.

Dancing
in the Kitchen

a few favorite salads

chickpea salad

chickpea salad

Chickpeas (a.k.a. garbanzo beans) have a fabulous flavor and are full of wonderful nutrients. This tan, round bean is a staple in my kitchen whether it's winter or summer. During the cooler months, I use these little nuggets in soups and stews. In summer, they are perfect for salad. As my children grow, and their taste buds mature, they enjoy bean salads more and more. Chickpea Salad is one of their favorites, and I must say, it's mine, too. This mouthwatering salad combines the most popular summer vegetables and herbs with a dressing of citrus juice and balsamic vinegar. If you sat at our dinner table, you would see me dancing in my chair and wriggling with joy, as I savor my first few bites. Chickpea Salad just has that effect on me. And, even though they may not show it on the outside, I think my kids are dancing on the inside.

4 cups cooked chickpeas (See cooking instructions on page 33.)
1/2 cup red onion, diced
1 cup corn, fresh or frozen (cooked in a small amount of water and cooled)
Cilantro leaves
Roasted Red Peppers (page 53), cubed

Dressing:
1 tablespoon olive oil
2 tablespoons lime juice
1 tablespoon balsamic vinegar
1 garlic clove, minced
Dash of sea salt

Place the chickpeas, red onion, corn, cilantro, and red peppers into a bowl. In another smaller bowl, whisk together the olive oil, lime juice, balsamic vinegar, garlic, and salt. Now add the dressing to the salad and stir well, coating all of the ingredients with the dressing. Let the salad sit for about 30 minutes, and then taste it to see if you need to adjust the flavor. This salad can stand alone as a meal when served with avocado. You can add it to a green salad, or serve it in a soft, warmed corn or flour tortilla. This is a perfect complement to a grain dish and steamed broccoli. With so much color and flavor, what more could you ask for?

roasted red peppers

roasted red peppers

My good friend Jamie's husband is of Italian descent. Many years ago, when Jamie and I would get together with our children for potluck lunches, she would bring this amazing side dish of Roasted Red Peppers. This can be served on bread, hummus, rice, scrambled eggs, or as a garnish for soups. I even use them inside my Nori Rolls (page 63). The bright red of the pepper and the green of the parsley or cilantro will feed the eye of anyone dining at your table, not to mention tantalize the taste buds.

3 red peppers
2 to 3 garlic cloves, very, very thinly sliced
1/8 teaspoon sea salt
2 to 3 tablespoons olive oil
Cilantro leaves or parsley (or a combination of both)

I have a gas stove, so it makes roasting the peppers easy. They can also be roasted under an oven broiler. Wash and dry the peppers and place them, on their sides, on the grate above one or two gas burners. Set the burner to a medium flame. As the flame darkens the skin of the peppers, turn the peppers so that another section can roast. Continue this process until most of each pepper has been browned. Now place the hot peppers into a paper bag, and fold over the opening so that the heat doesn't escape.

After about 15 minutes, take out one pepper at a time and place it on a cutting board or parchment paper. The soft, loose skin of the pepper is easy to remove with the scraping motion of a table knife. With the knife, remove all of the skin until the bright red flesh underneath is present. Be careful to not puncture the pepper.

Set the first pepper aside, take another pepper out of the bag, and follow the same process. After the last pepper is skinned, it's time to slice the peppers. Have a medium bowl handy as you make a slit in one of the red peppers. (There will be a sweet juice inside the pepper that you will want to save.) Once the slit has been made, turn the pepper over the bowl and allow the sweet juice to drain into the bowl. When all of the liquid is out, lengthen the slit from the top to the bottom of the pepper. Remove the stem of the pepper and a small area around it, plus the seeds. With a sharp knife, slice the pepper into very thin strips from top to bottom and place it into the bowl with the juice. Now do the same to the other two peppers. After all the peppers are drained, seeded, and sliced, add the garlic, salt, olive oil, and cilantro or parsley. Mix well. You now have a most flavorful garnish that will make you wish that red peppers were available all year long. This garnish can enhance just about any dish or dinner. Enjoy.

quinoa salad

quinoa salad

Quinoa has made its way into the news the past several years and has been given the title "South American Super Grain." It used to be a grain one would find only in health food stores, but as of late, you can find quinoa in most grocery stores. It is even served in many restaurants as an option for those who are gluten intolerant. Quinoa has a nutty flavor that is full of vegetarian protein, and I believe that this grain deserves a permanent spot on your pantry shelf. When it does find its way there, your body and your taste buds will be happy that it did. Quinoa Salad is one of my favorite summer salads. This salad has so many wonderful flavors and textures that you really will want to jump for joy. From the sweet tangerine juice to the dried, sweet and tart cranberries to the rich, crunchy cashews, this salad may just become another one of your favorites.

1 cup cooked quinoa, cooled (See cooking instructions below.)
1-1/4 cups water
Pinch of sea salt
1/2 cup cashews, coarsely chopped
1/4 cup dried cranberries, whole or coarsely chopped
2 scallions, thinly sliced
10 mint leaves (or more if you love the taste of mint), thinly sliced or minced

Cilantro leaves (as many as you wish)
Flat leaf parsley (as much as you wish), stems removed

Dressing:
1/4 cup tangerine juice
2 tablespoons lime juice
1 tablespoon olive oil
1/4 teaspoon sea salt

Soak 1 cup of quinoa in fresh water for 8 hours. After the soaking period, wash and rinse the quinoa many times and then strain out the water. Add the quinoa to a pot with the water and salt. Bring to a boil, cover the pot, and then turn down the heat to low. I have a flame tamer that I use regularly to help cook grains evenly on the bottom of the pot. So if you choose to use one, this is the time to place your pot on top of it. Allow the quinoa to cook for 35 minutes. Remove the pot from the heat and fluff the quinoa with a fork. Place the lid back on the pot, and let the quinoa cool. If you wish, after 10 minutes, you may place the hot quinoa into a bowl (preferably, a non-plastic bowl) and allow it to cool this way, fluffing occasionally.

Prepare the salad dressing by whisking all ingredients together in a bowl. Set aside. Put the cooled quinoa into a bowl. Add the remaining ingredients and stir lightly. Add the dressing and mix well. Let the salad sit for at least 30 minutes and then taste it, adjusting the flavor as needed. For a sweeter taste, use more tangerine juice, or for a tangier flavor, use more lime juice. You may also choose to use lemon instead of the lime. I like to serve Quinoa Salad with black beans and avocado. Perfection.

summer potato salad

summer potato salad

Memorial Day weekend, the Fourth of July, or a summer picnic in the park with my family would not be the same without Summer Potato Salad. We can usually find local corn and red peppers by the end of May, so on Memorial Day weekend, we have our first Summer Potato Salad of the year. With longer, warmer days, we are reminded that summer is just around the corner. As you know by now, potatoes are loved by the men in my life, and Summer Potato Salad is another way for them to get their fix. I add other veggies to the salad for me, so this way, we are all happy!

6 to 8 potatoes, quartered (I use Yukon gold potatoes, washed well with a vegetable brush.)

3 ears yellow or white corn, shucked and silks removed with a vegetable brush

4 celery stalks, sliced lengthwise and then thinly sliced

3 green onions, very thinly sliced (with roots and any wilted or yellow greens removed)

1/2 to 1 red pepper, diced

Parsley or cilantro leaves (as many as you wish)

1/4 to 1/2 cup mayonnaise or Vegenaise

2 teaspoons prepared mustard

1-1/4 teaspoon sea salt

1/8 teaspoon ground black pepper

Place the prepared potatoes in a large pot with 1 teaspoon salt and cover them with water. Turn on the heat and bring the water to a boil. Reduce the heat to low so that there are very few bubbles in the water. This allows the potatoes to cook slowly and keep their shape. When you can insert a fork easily into a potato, they are done. Very carefully, pour the water and potatoes into a colander, draining out the cooking water. Allow the potatoes to cool.

While the potatoes are cooling, cut the corn off the cobs, saving the cobs for Clear Broth (page 25). Place the corn in a skillet with a very small amount of water and a sprinkle of salt. Bring the water to a boil, and then reduce the heat to medium, stirring the corn occasionally as it cooks. After about 2 minutes, most of the water should have evaporated, but don't worry if there is still some left in the skillet. Place the corn on a plate to cool.

Next, put the celery, green onions, and red pepper into a bowl, and sprinkle with about a 1/4 teaspoon salt and 1/8 teaspoon ground pepper. Mix the seasonings throughout the vegetables, and let the vegetables sit for about 15 minutes.

When the potatoes are cool, use a paring knife to remove the skin; it will come off very easily. Cut the potatoes into bite-sized pieces. (I usually keep mine on the bigger side.) Place them into a bowl. The corn should be cooled by now, so it can be added to the potatoes along with the celery, onions, red pepper, and the parsley or cilantro.

Put the mayonnaise and mustard on top of all the vegetables. And now for the fun part! With clean hands, mix the mayonnaise or Vegenaise and mustard into the potato and vegetable mixture until everything is coated. Taste your salad to see if the flavors need adjusting. Does it need more salt, mustard, or black pepper? After you have adjusted the flavors, place the bowl into the fridge and allow the salad to cool for at least 1 hour. Welcome to summer!

black bean salad

black bean salad

Just looking at this salad brings me joy! With so many beautiful and contrasting colors, I can't help but admire each individual ingredient. When I eat Black Bean Salad, I feel very satisfied with its medley of flavors: sweet, sour, salty, and pungent. During the summer, this salad is found quite often in our fridge, and with many outdoor activities that keep me out of the kitchen, it's nice to come home to a meal that is already prepared. Remember, when you prepare black beans, make extra to use in other dishes. With their deep purple-black color, it doesn't take many vegetables to create an eye-catching dish.

1 cup cooked black beans (See cooking instructions on page 33.)
2 to 3 ears yellow corn, cut off the cob and cooked in a small amount of water
2 medium tomatoes (red, yellow, or orange for color), diced
1/2 small red onion, diced
Cilantro leaves (as many as you wish)
Jalapeño pepper (a few thin slices), minced

Dressing:
2 tablespoons lime juice
1 tablespoon olive oil
1/4 teaspoon sea salt
1 medium garlic clove, minced

Drain the beans, and place them in a bowl. When the corn is cool, add it to the bowl along with the tomatoes, onion, cilantro, and jalapeño pepper. In a separate bowl, combine the dressing ingredients, and whisk with a fork. Stir the dressing into the beans and vegetables. I use a rubber spatula to reach the dressing that runs to the bottom of the bowl. Stir occasionally over the next 30 minutes and then taste. At this point, adjust the flavor to your liking. This salad is always great served with slices of avocado on a bed of lettuce.

grains

Yes, there's controversy these days about eating grains, so it's up to you to decide if grain does your body good. Whole grains work for me, and I eat one kind or another every day. Brown rice is my favorite; the longer I chew, the sweeter it becomes. It seems to go well with whatever I make for dinner, and it also makes a delicious Soft Rice Porridge (page 107). There are many different types of brown rice: short grain, medium grain, long grain, sweet, jasmine, basmati, wild, forbidden black, red, and on and on. There are also white varieties.

Among my favorite grains are quinoa, amaranth, oats, einkorn (an ancient wheat), millet, polenta (ground corn), and buckwheat. I use some of these grains for flour and others for eating with our meals. I like them all and use them regularly, and they fit easily into any meal, any time of the day.

Cooking Instructions

What's the best way to prepare grains? My favorite way is to soak all grains for 8 to 12 hours before cooking. Generally, I soak 2 cups of grain for each meal. I place it in a pot and cover it with water. I give it a gentle stir to submerge all of the grain in the water. After the grain has soaked, I wash it at least three times and then drain it in a wire strainer.

For all types of brown rice, I pour 3 cups of clean filtered water into a pot with 1/8 teaspoon Himalayan salt or sea salt. I bring the water to a boil and then add the 2 cups of soaked, drained rice. After bringing the rice back up to a boil again, I place the lid on the pot, reduce the heat to low, and cook for 50 minutes. I stir the grain gently and then serve. I love to mix different rice varieties together. Basmati and jasmine have wonderful aromatic scents, and either one pairs nicely with any of the other brown rice varieties. However you choose to combine them will be delicious! Any leftovers can be stored in the fridge for several days, so they're available when you want to make a quick meal. Remember to chew!

Quinoa is a nutritional powerhouse. Its wonderful, nutty taste is one of my favorites. To prepare quinoa, I also soak it 8 to 12 hours. Wash it well and drain it after the soaking period. Then, for every 1 cup of quinoa, add 1-1/3 cups of water to a pot with a pinch of salt. Bring the water to a boil, add the drained quinoa, and bring the water back to a boil. Place a lid on the pot, reduce the heat to low, and cook for 30 minutes.

nori rolls

nori rolls

You might ask, "What are Nori Rolls?" During my macrobiotic training, "nori rolls" referred to a vegetarian version of sushi. Nori, a sea vegetable, is the outermost layer of a roll that contains rice and fillings. Once you get the hang of using a sushi mat, you can make any type of Nori Roll you like. The only thing that would hold you back is your imagination. Years ago, when I worked in the deli of our health food store, making Nori Rolls was one of the jobs I created for myself. I came up with some fun rolls that blended this Japanese food with the flavors of many countries. I tried Mexican, Greek, Italian, American, and Middle Eastern foods inside my rolls, and they were a hit. This is a fantastic way to wrap up any of your favorite foods. The sky's the limit on what you create.

> **Brown or white rice (See cooking instructions on page 61.)**
> **Sushi mat**
> **Toasted nori or untoasted nori that you toast yourself**
> **Fillings of your choice**

Prepare the rice, and allow it to cool completely. For Nori Rolls, you can use short- or medium-grain brown rice, white sushi rice, or basmati rice—actually, almost any type of rice you'd like. The traditional Japanese rice in any type of sushi is short-grain white rice, which is called sushi rice.

I recommend buying toasted nori, as it makes rolling easier and quicker. I buy 50-sheet packs of nori, so I can make lots and lots of rolls. Eating nori plain or as a garnish with soup or grain is a great way to get extra nutrients.

If at first you don't succeed, try try again! It may take several attempts to get the hang of creating this artistic food, but I promise it is well worth it. Consider it practice in *not* being perfect.

Place your sushi mat on a cutting board or a clean countertop. Be sure the bamboo strands in the sushi mat are positioned horizontally. Take a sheet of nori, noticing that it has a rough side and a smooth side, and place it on the sushi mat with the rough side up. Make sure the length of the nori runs parallel to the bamboo strands. Have your cooked rice within easy reach, along with a small bowl of water for dipping your fingertips to keep the rice from sticking to them. With a spoon, scoop the rice onto the nori. Dip your fingertips into the water, shaking off any excess. Press the rice gently onto the nori while spreading it across the sheet. Add more rice, as needed, and dip your fingertips in the water to keep the rice from sticking. As shown in photo 1, start from the end closest to you and cover the nori with a layer of rice about 1/8-inch thick, leaving a 1-1/2-inch wide strip of nori uncovered at the top.

Photo 1. Rice layered on nori with 1-1/2-inch space at top

Now comes the tough part. (Not really! It's the fun part!) What do you want to put inside? Let's say I'm making a Mexican-type Nori Roll. What would I want to put inside? Salsa comes to mind. How about avocado, beans, and maybe cheese? So let's put these Mexican rolls together!

As shown in photo 2, add your fillings on top of the rice, one at a time, about one-third of the way from the edge of the nori that is closest to you. Starting on the left or right side, make a horizontal line of salsa that reaches from one side to the other. The first time you attempt to make Nori Rolls, use small amounts of each filling. If you use too much, it will be difficult to roll. Next, on top of the salsa, add pinto beans or black beans horizontally. As an avocado lover, I add avocado next. (The avocado is easier to work with if it's cut into thin strips.) As a finishing touch, I add sliced cheese either right next to the avocado or on top of it.

Photo 2. Fillings laid horizontally on rice

Great job! That part is done. The final and trickiest part is rolling up the nori. As shown in photo 3, place your thumbs underneath the sushi mat on the side closest to your body and lift it slightly. Place your other fingers on the backside of the fillings to hold them in place. Now with your thumbs, roll the edge of the sushi mat up and over the fillings, without smashing them. This part takes some practice.

Photo 3. Using a sushi mat to roll the nori sheet

The edge of the nori that was closest to you should now be wrapped once around the fillings. Tuck the nori edges horizontally, and then move the part of the sushi mat closest to you out of the way. With your thumbs on the front side of the roll, directly touching the nori, and your fingers on the back, continue to roll the nori until you come to the 1-1/2-inch strip that has no rice on it. Hold the roll in place with one hand, and with other hand, dip you fingertips into the water and gently wet the whole horizontal strip. Take care not to use too much water because the nori will compress, making it hard to close the roll.

With the strip damp, finish rolling the nori onto the strip to "glue" it onto the back of the roll. Gently rock the roll back and forth to seal the edge. Remove the sushi mat. Slice the Nori Roll into rounds, or cut it in half on a slight diagonal to showcase the contents of your roll. For my kids' lunches, I slice Nori Rolls into bite-sized rounds so they can share them with their friends. If I'm traveling, I either leave the Nori Rolls whole or slice them in half and wrap the whole roll in parchment paper. Rubber bands at each end of the roll help to keep the parchment paper in place.

Here are some suggested combinations, but the possibilities are endless:

- Hummus, olives, and feta cheese
- Mayonnaise, turkey, tomato, cheese, and lettuce strips
- Scrambled eggs, cheese, salsa, and avocado (for breakfast, lunch, or dinner!)
- Vegenaise, green onion, avocado, and Roasted Red Peppers (page 53)
- Tomato sauce, olives, Italian cheese, and arugula

polenta

polenta

Polenta is a creamy corn dish that my whole family loves. The simplicity of this recipe and its versatility mean you can enjoy it many different ways. In California, we get the season's first organic corn in May. When I make this dish with the season's first corn, I'm reminded that summer is on its way, school vacation is almost here, and there will be more time to spend with my children and my friends.

> **1 tablespoon olive oil**
> **1/2 brown onion, diced**
> **5 cups water**
> **3/4 teaspoon sea salt**
> **1-1/2 cups polenta (a.k.a. corn grits)**
> **4 to 6 ears yellow, white, or bicolored corn, grated off the cob (optional)**

Heat the olive oil and onions in a saucepan, and sauté until the onion becomes translucent. Add the water and salt to the onions, and bring to a boil. Reduce the heat to medium, and very slowly pour the polenta into the water, stirring constantly. Stir the polenta for a few minutes while the corn absorbs the water. Now place a lid on the pot, reduce the heat to low, and cook the grits for 20 minutes. Stir the polenta every 5 minutes or so.

After 20 minutes, stir the grated corn into the polenta. Cook another 10 minutes, stirring occasionally.

If you prefer soft polenta, then serve it now. My family loves soft polenta topped with flax seed oil, green onions, and soy sauce. Save the uneaten portion of the polenta in a baking dish. It will become firm as it cools. Once the polenta has cooled, cover and place the polenta in the fridge until you are ready to use it.

When that time comes, cut the polenta into square or triangular pieces. Heat a skillet on medium heat and then add some olive oil. Now place the cut polenta into the skillet and cook one side until it is browned. Flip it over to brown the other side, and it is ready to be served. What a great way to get two meals out of one grain preparation!

Variations:

- For dinner, top polenta with Roasted Red Peppers (page 53), pasta sauce, or pesto.
- For breakfast, top with maple syrup, soy sauce, oil, or nuts.

millet potage

millet potage

I love millet, and it's also one of the grains I use in my freshly ground four-grain flour mix. Millet Potage is a go-to recipe when you might not be sure what to make for dinner but are hungry for something delicious and filling. Millet Potage can be made as a hearty breakfast, a savory lunch, or a simple dinner. I make Millet Potage with winter squash, carrots, corn, and cabbage, but you can make it with any one of these or a combination of two or three vegetables.

- 1 cup millet, soaked for 8 to 12 hours
- 1 onion, diced
- 2 teaspoons olive oil
- 1 cup winter squash, cubed and skin removed
- 1 cup carrots, sliced into 1/2-inch circles
- 1 cup corn, fresh or frozen
- 1 cup green cabbage, cubed
- 4 cups water
- 1/2 teaspoon sea salt

After the millet has soaked for 8 to 12 hours, wash it several times and drain the excess water. In a medium pot, sauté the onion in the olive oil. After the onion becomes translucent, add the squash, carrots, corn, and cabbage. Then add the water, millet, and salt. Bring the water to a boil, place a lid on the pot, reduce the heat to low, and cook for 30 minutes. Green onions and toasted pumpkin seeds make a super garnish on top of this millet meal, as does a drizzle of soy sauce.

Dancing
in the Kitchen

other favorites

mexican lasagna

mexican lasagna

I love the flavors in Mexican food, and not being a fan of traditional Italian lasagna, I felt there had to be a way to make something similar to lasagna but with a Mexican flair. That's how my Mexican Lasagna came to be. I put cheese on half of the lasagna before baking, so Jimbo can have his vegan half. Adding a fried egg helps me feel physically satisfied after one of these meals. Every one of my kids loves this meal. We add egg, slices of avocado, and salsa for a feeling of family happiness!

1 medium onion, chopped

1 to 3 teaspoons olive oil

1/8 to 1/4 jalapeño pepper, diced (including some of the seeds)

1 cup corn, fresh or frozen

3 cups water (or enough to create the consistency of a medium-thick soup)

2 tablespoons tomato paste

1/2 teaspoon sea salt

3 to 4 cups cooked pinto beans
(See cooking instructions on page 33.)

1 to 2 garlic cloves, minced

Cilantro leaves (as many as you wish)

Corn tortillas (for layering)

Grated cheese (optional)

Brown rice (optional)

Preheat the oven to 350 degrees. In a large pot, sauté the onion in olive oil until translucent. Add the jalapeño pepper to the pot. After a few minutes, add the corn, giving it a light stir. Now add the water, tomato paste, and salt. Bring the mixture to a light boil, and then turn down the heat to simmer. Add the cooked pinto beans, garlic, and cilantro, mixing the ingredients together well. Taste the sauce and adjust its flavor if needed. Once your sauce is ready, it's time to build your lasagna.

Cut the tortillas in half, and place a layer in a casserole dish to cover the bottom completely. If your dish is rectangular, the cut edge will be placed along the outside edge of the dish. You can use whole tortillas in the center of the pan. If you choose to use brown rice, place a thin layer on top of the tortillas. If you wish, cheese can be placed on top of the rice. I sometimes use just a small amount for flavor, but add as much as you like. Now scoop the pinto bean "sauce" on top of the tortillas, adding enough to cover all of the rice or tortillas. Cut more tortillas to make a second layer on top of the sauce. Once these tortillas are in place, again add sauce to cover these tortillas. If you'd like, you can add more grated cheese to top off the sauce. Cover your baking dish, and place it in the oven. Bake for 25 minutes or until the sauce bubbles around the edges. Remove the lasagna from the oven, and let it rest for 30 minutes before cutting and serving. This resting time allows the tortillas to absorb the liquid in the sauce and set.

If your week is busy and getting dinner together is a struggle, make your sauce ahead of time. Let it cool and then build your lasagna. Cover and store the lasagna in the fridge until you are ready to bake it. With glassware, which is what I use most often, if it's been in the refrigerator, I put the lasagna in the oven while the oven is preheating so as not to shock the glass. This way, the glass has time to adjust slowly to the rising temperature.

salsa

salsa

While working at our family's health food store, Jimbo's...Naturally! some 30 years ago, I longed to make a traditional Mexican salsa to sell in the deli. Javier, a friend of Jimbo's, was from Mexico, so I asked him if he had a salsa recipe he'd be willing to share with me. The funny thing is, the recipe he gave me, which is the one his mother makes, is just like the recipe advice I'm suggesting to you. Her recipe listed the ingredients, but I had to figure out the proportions that worked best for me. I give you my proportions here, but again, adjust the salsa to incorporate more of your favorite flavors. In the winter when tomatoes are not in season, I use Satsuma tangerines for a spectacular-tasting salsa!

4 tomatoes (red, yellow, or orange for color), diced and stems removed
1/3 cup red onion, finely diced
Juice of 1 lime
1/4 teaspoon sea salt
1/8 to 1/4 jalapeño pepper
1 garlic clove, minced
Cilantro leaves

Prepare all of the ingredients and place in a bowl, mixing well. Let sit for 15 minutes before adjusting the flavor. The best salsa is your own.

sweets

soaked and dried nuts

I use nuts or Almond Milk (page 79) in many of my sweet recipes. Soaking and drying nuts and seeds at a low temperature resonated with me from the very moment I heard about it. Why? With more and more information coming out about the sensitive oils in nuts and seeds, it makes sense to me to be gentle when heating them and to avoid denaturing the oils by roasting them at a high temperature. I love the sweetness and crispness of nuts prepared this way.

Instructions

Place 4 cups of nuts or seeds in a bowl with water to cover and 1 teaspoon of salt. Soak the nuts or seeds for 12 hours. I usually start the soaking process in the early evening or early morning, so I'm still awake when it's time to dry the nuts or seeds in the oven. After soaking, rinse the nuts very well (a few times), and place them in a strainer to allow the excess water to drain. Preheat the oven to its lowest temperature setting. I never invested in a dehydrator because my oven's lowest temperature is 130 degrees. There are ovens with lower temperature settings than mine, but no matter what your oven's lowest setting is, it will work.

Line a cookie sheet with parchment paper, spread the nuts across the paper, and place the cookie sheet in the oven. Walnuts and pecans take 8 to 12 hours to dry. Almonds can take up to 24 hours, depending on how low the temperature is in your oven. Seeds dry more quickly than nuts, usually in 4 to 6 hours. To test for doneness, take a few nuts or seeds out of the oven, let them cool, and then taste them. If they are crispy enough for you, they are done. If not, continue drying until they are.

When they're finished, remove them from the oven and allow them to cool completely. Store them in a glass jar in your cupboard. They are great as a snack, mixed with dried fruit, in salads, in cookies, or on top of cold or hot cereal. Really, they are delicious any way you choose to eat them.

almond milk

almond milk

Almond Milk is a favorite of mine! I use it as a substitute in any recipe that calls for cow's milk. I use it for pancakes, hot and cold cereals, cakes, and puddings. It is very easy to make and lasts for one week in the fridge.

3/4 cup raw almonds
Water for soaking
4 cups water

Nut milk bag (available at health food stores or online)
Clean glass jar for storage

Place the almonds in a bowl, and cover them with water. Almonds double in size during soaking, so be sure the bowl is large enough to allow for this expansion. Soak the almonds for 8 to 12 hours to start the sprouting process. After soaking, rinse the almonds a few times. Now you are ready to make your Almond Milk.

At this point, you have two options: You can place the almonds in a blender with the 4 cups of water, and blend for 2 minutes on high speed. Or, for a milk that's whiter in color, you can add enough water to just cover the almonds and then add boiling water to create a water temperature similar to that of hot tea. Let the almonds sit in the hot water until the water cools. Then rinse the almonds twice. After rinsing, place them in the blender with the 4 cups of water, and blend for 2 minutes. This second option removes a bit more of the color from the almond skins so that the milk is a little bit whiter.

Pour the blended Almond Milk into a nut milk bag over a bowl or a 4-cup Pyrex measuring cup. With clean hands, squeeze the nut milk bag, allowing all the milk to come out and into the container. Squeeze as hard as you can to remove as much milk as possible. Nut milk bags do a fabulous job of straining out the nut meal, and they are easy to wash and dry. I replace my bags only a couple of times a year, and I make a lot of nut milk. Many health food stores carry them, or you can find them online. They are very handy to have in your kitchen. If you can't locate a nut milk bag, try using cheesecloth, folded several times, to prevent the meal from making its way into your milk. Or, you can try a very fine-mesh strainer. With the backside of a large metal spoon, press the almond meal against the strainer, removing most of the milk. Transfer the milk into a quart jar and store it in the refrigerator for up to a week.

If you have children who are not fond of the taste of Almond Milk, here is a simple way to transition them to Almond Milk: Start by replacing one-quarter of their favorite milk with Almond Milk. After a while, replace one-half of their favorite milk with the Almond Milk. Continue this process until your child has transitioned completely to Almond Milk.

Almonds are not the only nut used for milk. Nut milk can be made from cashews, pecans, macadamia nuts, pumpkin seeds, sesame seeds, and coconuts. I sometimes combine 1/2 cup of almonds with 1/4 cup of another variety of nut to make Almond Milk. Play around with the flavors and the nutritional profile until you find what you like. Doing so is a great way to create different-tasting nut milks.

For those of you who like a sweeter nut milk, feel free to add honey, maple syrup, coconut sugar, dates, or maybe a splash of vanilla. This should do the trick. Nut milk may separate while in the refrigerator, so give it a gentle shake before using.

pumpkin pie filling

pumpkin pie filling

When my boys started elementary school, I had to come up with ways to keep them eating their own lunches because I didn't want them trading with other kids for less healthy food. I think their homemade lunches many times were the envy of the other kids, who often had processed or packaged foods. On most school days, my boys came home with empty containers.

I look forward to fall and the sweet vegetables that are harvested during this time of year. Pumpkins and squashes are abundant, and they are the ones I look forward to the most because it means pumpkin pudding and pumpkin pie. Kabocha (Japanese) pumpkin, butternut, or buttercup squashes are the sweetest squashes I've found. I use them for pies because they are so sweet that I don't need to use as much maple syrup in my recipe. Sugar pie pumpkins work well, too, but you will want to use the full amount of sweetener that's called for in this recipe.

3-1/2 cups cooked squash or pumpkin, cooled
1/4 cup creamy almond butter
1/4 cup arrowroot powder (a thickener available at health food stores)
1/4 to 3/4 cup maple syrup (Use the lesser amount with a sweeter pumpkin or squash.)
3/4 cup or more Almond Milk (page 79)

1/4 teaspoon sea salt
1/4 teaspoon ground cloves
1/4 teaspoon ground ginger
1/8 teaspoon ground nutmeg
1/2 to 1 teaspoon ground cinnamon
2 teaspoons pure vanilla extract
1 9-inch piecrust (optional)

Preheat the oven to 350 degrees. Rinse the outside of the pumpkin or squash to wash off any dirt. Pat dry. With a heavy knife, cut the pumpkin in half through the center pole, stem to base. Try to cut it into even halves, so the two pieces will cook in the same amount of time. Scoop out the seeds, using a metal spoon. Place the pumpkin halves on a cookie sheet with cut sides down. I line the cookie sheet with unbleached parchment paper for easy cleanup. Place the cookie sheet in the oven, and bake the squash for 45 to 75 minutes, until you can press down on the skin and it gives quite easily. Allow the pumpkin to cool until you can touch it without burning your hands. Sometimes, I cook the pumpkin in the evening, so it can cool overnight on the cookie sheet. In the morning, it's ready to be made into pie filling. Take note of how moist the pumpkin is after it's done cooking and cooling. This will help you determine how much Almond Milk to add. Over my many years of making Pumpkin Pie Filling, I have found that water content varies among different varieties of pumpkins and squashes and from season to season.

Flip the pumpkin over, scoop out the flesh, and place it into a large bowl. Before adding the remaining ingredients, taste the pumpkin. Is it sweet? If it is, start off with the lesser amount of sweetener (1/4 cup). Now add the remaining ingredients to the bowl of pumpkin and mix well. If the pumpkin mixture seems dry, add more Almond Milk. Taste the mixture to determine whether you need to add more sweetener. Place half of the pumpkin mixture into a blender, and blend until creamy. If it seems too thick to blend, add small amounts of Almond Milk until you get a nice, creamy consistency. For pumpkin pudding, the mixture should be thinner than for pumpkin pie, so add more Almond Milk as needed. Drier pumpkins or squashes may need up to 2 cups of Almond Milk. Place the pureed pumpkin into a bowl, and then blend the other half of the mixture. Add this batch to the first batch and mix well. You should have a creamy and slightly thick pumpkin puree.

To make a pumpkin pie, which I usually do only during the holidays, pour the puree into a piecrust, and bake at 350 degrees for about 45 minutes, until the top is lightly browned.

To make pumpkin pudding, pour this mixture into a Pyrex baking dish and bake for about 45 minutes. For my kids' lunches, I use the pudding method because I don't always want to make a piecrust.

Allow the pudding or pie to cool, and then cover and store it in the fridge. For lunch boxes, I have an assortment of small, metal containers that I use for pudding. This pudding is delicious topped with Almond Créme (page 89).

coconut cookies

coconut cookies

Over the years, I've made many different kinds of cookies for my family, and Coconut Cookies have become a staple in our house. I love combining the nuts, dried fruits, and spices to make a completely different-tasting cookie. I've used pecans, cashews, almonds, and filberts in place of pistachios. Chocolate chips make a nice substitute for the cranberries, as do dried wild blueberries, chopped dates, or dried apricots. I love the refreshing flavor of cardamom, so I use it sometimes in place of cinnamon. Let your imagination run wild to create something wonderful and delicious. I keep a cookie jar in my car, and it doesn't take long before the jar is empty.

1/4 cup coconut oil (or a combination of light olive oil and coconut oil)
1/4 cup rice syrup
1/4 cup maple syrup
1/4 teaspoon sea salt
2 teaspoons pure vanilla extract
1/3 cup shredded coconut
1/2 cup pistachios, chopped
1/3 cup dried cranberries, chopped
1 cup flour*
3/4 cup oatmeal, finely ground (Pulse grind in a coffee grinder or blender.)
3/4 teaspoon baking powder
1/2 teaspoon ground cinnamon

Preheat the oven to 350 degrees. Melt the coconut oil in a pan on low heat, and then transfer it to a bowl. Add the rice syrup, maple syrup, salt, and vanilla to the coconut oil and whisk together. Stir in the shredded coconut, pistachios, and cranberries. In a separate bowl, combine the flour, oatmeal, baking powder, and cinnamon. Now combine the wet and dry ingredients, mixing well.

Line a cookie sheet with parchment paper, and spoon about 1 tablespoon of cookie dough per cookie onto the sheet. Once all of the cookie dough has been placed onto the cookie sheet, put the cookie sheet into the oven. Bake for about 25 minutes or until golden brown. Halfway through the baking, you may want to turn the tray around to be sure the cookies bake evenly.

*You can use white flour, whole wheat pastry flour, or gluten-free flour. I like to grind equal parts millet, buckwheat, brown rice, and einkorn (an ancient wheat), which I keep in a glass jar and use throughout the week. Years ago, I invested in a flour mill, and I love being able to grind any grain I want into flour. I stick mostly with the grain combination mentioned above because, to me, it makes great-tasting cakes, cookies, and sweet breads that also have a wonderful texture.

chocolate pudding

chocolate pudding

Creamy, decadent, and dairy free. Need I say more?

2-3/4 cups water
1/4 teaspoon sea salt
1-3/4 tablespoons agar flakes (a vegan gelling agent)
2 tablespoons kudzu root powder (as a thickener)

2 tablespoons water
1/2 cup rice syrup
1/2 cup maple syrup
6 tablespoons cocoa powder
1/3 cup creamy almond butter
2 teaspoons pure vanilla extract

In a saucepan, combine the water, salt, and agar, and let set for 10 minutes, allowing the agar to soften. Don't worry if you leave it longer; it will be fine. Bring the liquid to a boil, whisking continuously. Once the mixture boils, lower the heat to simmer, and give the agar about 10 minutes to completely dissolve, whisking occasionally. Remove any agar that attaches to the sides of the saucepan. While the agar is simmering, dissolve the kudzu in a small bowl with 2 tablespoons water. Kudzu looks like small, soft, white rocks, so each tablespoon will look more like a heaping tablespoon. In a separate bowl, combine the rice syrup, maple syrup, and cocoa, mixing well.

After the agar is dissolved and no flakes are visible in the pot, add the kudzu and water. Be sure to give the kudzu mixture a quick stir since kudzu sinks to the bottom of the bowl when it sits. When adding the kudzu to the pot, be sure to whisk continuously to prevent lumps from forming. Once the kudzu is blended and the water becomes clear, add the almond butter, thoroughly mixing it into the liquid.

Now add the cocoa mixture, and whisk continuously while bringing the pudding up to a low boil. When boiling is evident, return the heat to simmer, and cook for a few minutes. Don't be concerned if the pudding becomes thinner as it cooks; this is normal.

Turn off the heat and stir in the vanilla. If you want a really creamy pudding, pour the pudding through a stainless steel, fine-mesh strainer into a glass bowl to remove any almond skins that may be present in the almond butter. As the pudding cools, whisk often to keep it smooth. The pudding thickens as it cools to room temperature. If it seems too thick at room temperature, add small amounts of boiling water until you have the consistency you like. Once it is at room temperature, pour the pudding into glass containers, cover, and store them in the fridge. The pudding will last two weeks.

Variations:

- Any nut butter works for this recipe. Peanut butter is a fabulous choice as well as hazelnut butter.
- For less sweetness, reduce the maple syrup and increase the rice syrup. For more sweetness, increase the maple syrup and reduce the rice syrup.
- There are many organic flavorings you can use in place of the vanilla extract. I often use coffee instead of the water to make a mocha pudding that is also delicious.
- I like my puddings softer than firm, but if you like a thicker pudding, reduce the water to 2-1/2 cups. Also, instead of stirring as the pudding cools, pour the pudding directly into the glass containers and let it cool undisturbed. It will be nice and thick. (Just *try* keeping this in the house!)

lemon tangerine pudding

lemon tangerine pudding

I love Lemon Tangerine Pudding as much as my kids love Chocolate Pudding (page 85). The sweet-and-sour taste has my taste buds doing somersaults, and I can tell my liver loves it, too. Change the recipe using different combinations of lemon, lime, and tangerine juices to create different amounts of zing!

> **2 cups water**
> **3/4 teaspoon agar powder, not flakes (a vegan gelling agent)***
> **1/4 cup arrowroot powder (as a thickener)**
> **1/4 teaspoon sea salt**
> **3/4 cup juice, tangerine and lemon combined (your choice on how much of each)**
> **3/4 cup rice syrup**
> **1/4 cup maple syrup**
> **Zest of 1 lemon**
> **1/2 teaspoon pure vanilla extract**

In a pan, combine the water, agar powder, arrowroot powder, and salt. Bring to a boil on medium heat, stirring continuously. When the mixture becomes thick and translucent, add the juices, and whisk until all ingredients are blended, smooth, and creamy.

Next add the syrups, whisking continuously while bringing the pudding to just below a boil. Reduce the heat to low and allow the pudding to simmer for a few minutes, stirring occasionally.

Turn off the heat and stir in the lemon zest and vanilla. Once all the ingredients are blended together, pour the pudding into glass jars for storage. Cool the pudding to room temperature before placing it in the refrigerator. Lemon Tangerine Pudding lasts up to two weeks.

*Agar powder is more concentrated than agar flakes, and it dissolves very quickly. It is more expensive than the flakes, but you use much less of it to get the thickness you need for puddings. You can order agar powder through your health food store or online from macrobiotic websites. Some herb stores carry it as well. If you don't have agar powder, substitute an equal amount of unflavored gelatin powder.

almond créme

almond créme

For many years, Almond Créme has served as our "whipped cream" atop pies, cakes, puddings, and fresh fruit. I hope you find this fluffy topping as dreamy as my family does.

3/4 cup almonds
Water for soaking
3 cups water
2 tablespoons kudzu root powder
(as a thickener)
2 tablespoons water

1 teaspoon agar flakes (a vegan gelling agent)
1-1/4 cups water
1/4 teaspoon sea salt
4 tablespoons maple syrup
2 to 3 teaspoons pure vanilla extract

Place the almonds in a bowl, and cover them with water. Almonds double in size during soaking, so be sure the bowl is large enough to allow for this expansion. Soak the almonds for 8 to 12 hours to start the sprouting process. After soaking, rinse the almonds a few times. Blend the soaked almonds with the 3 cups of water. Strain out the almond meal as you would for Almond Milk (page 79), using a nut milk bag or fine-mesh strainer.

In a small bowl, dissolve the kudzu with 2 tablespoons of water. Kudzu looks like small, soft, white rocks, so each tablespoon will look more like a heaping tablespoon.

Next, place the agar, 1-1/4 cups water, and salt into a pot. Let the agar soften in the water for 10 minutes. Bring the ingredients to a boil on a medium-high heat, stirring continuously. Once the liquid boils, reduce the heat to simmer, and cook the mixture until the agar dissolves (approximately 10 minutes). Continue to stir the pot often, removing any agar that sticks to the sides.

Once the agar has dissolved, add the Almond Milk and maple syrup to the pot, whisking to blend everything together. While stirring continuously, bring the ingredients to just below a boil. Give the kudzu mixture a quick stir before adding it to the pot since kudzu settles to the bottom of the bowl when it sits. Whisk quickly and continuously while adding the kudzu. The mixture will begin to thicken. Once it has thickened, allow it to simmer for a few minutes.

Turn off the heat and add the vanilla, whisking until it is mixed in. If the kudzu contains lumps that cannot be smoothed out with a whisk, pour the mixture through a fine-mesh, stainless steel strainer, pressing out lumps with the back of a spoon. Place the Almond Créme into a glass bowl, whisking it occasionally as it cools to room temperature. Store Almond Créme in glass jars, and keep it refrigerated. It will keep for one week. Let a dollop of this luscious topping bring a fluffy joyfulness to any dessert or fruit bowl—enjoy!

peanut butter cookies

peanut butter cookies

Who doesn't love Peanut Butter Cookies? As a child, I remember fall days when my family would remain in our summer cabin, and we kids would take a bus to and from school every day. Taking the bus for a few weeks at the beginning of the school year was always an exciting adventure for me. I loved the Indian Summer, with very cool mornings and very hot afternoons. As we walked down the dusty, dirt road after the school bus dropped us off, I'd be thinking about the after-school snack my mom would have waiting for us. My very favorite snack was Peanut Butter Cookies with a glass of milk. I have continued this heart-warming tradition with my children, and on a fall day in San Diego when the Santa Ana winds blow, my kids often find a plate of Peanut Butter Cookies waiting for them when they get home from school.

1/2 cup peanut butter, creamy or chunky

1/4 cup oil (I combine equal parts light olive oil and coconut oil.)

1/2 cup maple syrup

2 teaspoons pure vanilla extract

1/4 teaspoon sea salt

3/4 cup oatmeal, finely ground (Pulse grind in a coffee grinder or blender.)

1/4 cup shredded coconut (optional)

1-1/3 cups flour

Preheat the oven to 350 degrees. Place the peanut butter, oil, maple syrup, vanilla, and salt in a bowl and mix well. Stir in the oatmeal and coconut. Add the flour, stirring gently, but thoroughly. With clean hands and a spoon, scoop some of the dough into your hands, and roll gently to form a ball about 1-1/2 inches in diameter. Place the balls on a cookie sheet lined with parchment paper. Then, dip a fork into flour and press it onto the top of each ball, making an imprint. Turn the fork about 90 degrees, and make another imprint that crisscrosses the first. Continue this process until all the cookies have imprints. Place the cookies into the oven, and bake until they're golden brown, approximately 20 minutes. Let the cookies cool, and store them in a glass jar or a container of your choice. Protein and deliciousness in every bite! These cookies will disappear fast, so get used to making them often!

apple crisp

apple crisp

The new fall crop of apples arrives in San Diego around the end of August. On those last days of the month, I scan the grocery store, searching for these round, red beauties. Once I see them, I have to eat one! The first bite and the next are mouthwatering. The wheels in my head start turning, and I find myself daydreaming about Apple Crisp. Signals are sent to my brain that fall is about to arrive, my favorite time of year.

Apple Crisp can be made year-round with any fruit or fruit combination you choose. The topping stays the same, and only the filling changes. So if you have a plum tree or an apricot tree, use the fruit for a crisp. Your house will never smell better!

Fruit base:
6 apples, peeled, quartered, seeds removed, and sliced 1/8-inch thick
3 to 4 tablespoons maple syrup (or sweetener of your choice)
Sprinkle of sea salt
1/4 teaspoon (or more if you'd like) ground cinnamon

Topping:
3/4 cup flour
1 cup oatmeal, finely ground (Pulse grind in a coffee grinder or blender.)
1/8 teaspoon sea salt
Dash of ground nutmeg
1/4 cup oil
2 tablespoons maple syrup
2 teaspoons pure vanilla extract

Preheat the oven to 350 degrees. Mix the apples, syrup, salt, and cinnamon together in a bowl. In a separate bowl, mix the flour, oatmeal, salt, and nutmeg. Add the oil to the flour mixture, and mix together with your fingertips, rubbing gently to mix in the oil. In a small bowl, combine the syrup and vanilla, and add it to the flour mixture. Use your fingertips to mix the syrup through the flour. Once it's all blended together, it's time to construct the crisp.

Place the prepared apples (or other fruit) in the bottom of a glass baking dish. A Pyrex dish works well. Sprinkle the topping evenly over the apples until they are completely covered. Covering the apples seals in the steam, allowing them to cook evenly.

Place the pan in the oven, and bake for about 45 minutes. Insert a fork into the center of the crisp. If the fork easily penetrates the apples, the crisp is done. I prefer glass baking dishes because I can watch for the juice that forms and begins to bubble. When the juice begins to bubble, I know it's about time to check the apples. Remove the crisp from the oven, and let it cool before storing in the refrigerator.

Variations:

- Try serving the crisp with Almond Créme (page 89), whipped cream, or ice cream (dairy or nondairy), especially when it's still warm. Remember to enjoy every bite knowing that fall is coming!
- Pears make a wonderful crisp, too and require less time to bake. Instead of cinnamon mixed into the fruit, use a couple of dashes of nutmeg. It's heavenly!
- Fresh and in-season blueberries are phenomenal options as well, and they are less expensive when they're in season. Frozen berries can be used, but you can't beat fresh! Pick through the fresh blueberries to remove any that are old or soft. Wash and drain them well. Now mix the syrup, salt, cinnamon, and 1 teaspoon of arrowroot powder into the blueberries. As the blueberries cook, they create a lot of juice, so arrowroot thickens the juice as it bakes, creating a fruity sauce. This recipe is a perfect way to show off harvested fruit any time of the year.

date bars

date bars

We are lucky to live in California where temperatures allow for dates to grow in abundance! One of the first gifts Jimbo gave me was a Barhi date branch. I watched and waited as the days passed, with one or two dates ripening each day. What a delicious treat. Dates are another one of the fruits I look forward to in the fall! I feel blessed to live in a state where so much wonderful food is grown, and we have a growing season that lasts all year. It's paradise. These date bars need no added sweetener. They're perfect just the way they are.

Filling:
1-1/4 cups Medjool dates, pitted and chopped
1/4 to 1/2 teaspoon ground cinnamon
Pinch of sea salt
1/4 cup water, if the dates are dry or 2 tablespoons if the dates are fresh

Topping for top and bottom:
1 cup oatmeal, finely ground (Pulse grind in a coffee grinder or blender.)

3/4 cup flour
1/8 teaspoon sea salt
1/8 teaspoon (or more) nutmeg
1/4 cup shredded or flaked coconut (optional)
1/4 cup oil (I use either light olive oil or coconut oil or a 50/50 blend.)
2 tablespoons water
2 teaspoons pure vanilla extract

Preheat the oven to 350 degrees. Place the dates, cinnamon, salt, and water into a saucepan. Simmer the ingredients at a low temperature, with the lid on, until all of the water has been absorbed. Stir occasionally, over 10 minutes, as a thick paste is created.

In a bowl, mix the oatmeal, flour, salt, nutmeg, and coconut. Add the oil to the flour mixture, using your fingertips to gently massage the oil into flour to create a crumble. In a small bowl, mix the water and vanilla. Add it to the flour mixture, and again, gently mix using your fingertips to create a crumble. Press half of the crumble into the bottom of a baking dish, covering it completely. Next, spoon the date paste onto the pressed crumble and gently spread it out. To avoid disrupting the crumble layer, spoon the date paste onto different areas of the crumble, so it's easier to spread. Sprinkle the other half of the crumble over the date paste until it's mostly covered. Now sprinkle on the coconut. The crumble and coconut may not cover all of the date paste, but that is just fine. Leaving some of it uncovered looks nice. Bake for 20 to 25 minutes or until the topping is golden brown. These bars make a nice fall or winter treat when fresh fruit is not available. They're even more enjoyable when savored with a nice cup of tea.

Variations:

- I've had loads of fun with this recipe, making all different types of dried fruit bars including fig, apricot, prune, and many other dried fruit combinations.
- Adding a small amount of dried blueberries or cherries to dried apricots is quite tasty.
- Nuts can be added to the topping as well as other spices such as clove, ginger, cardamom, or allspice.

almond cookies

almond cookies

This is a fantastic cookie for dipping in coffee, tea, milk, or just about anything. I started make these cookies for my children when they were teething, and we all got to enjoy their wonderful flavor. This is not a very sweet cookie, but you can change that by the type of sweetener you use. They last for weeks in a glass jar and seem to get sweeter as they sit.

> **1-1/2 cups almonds, finely ground (Grind in a blender.)**
> **1/4 cup shredded coconut (optional)**
> **1/2 teaspoon ground cinnamon**
> **1/8 teaspoon sea salt**
> **1/3 cup water**
> **2 teaspoons pure vanilla extract**
> **1/2 cup rice syrup (or a sweetener of your choice)**
> **1-1/2 cups flour**
> **1 to 2 tablespoons unrefined sugar or maple sugar (optional)**

Preheat the oven to 350 degrees. Mix together the almonds, coconut, cinnamon, and salt in a medium-sized bowl. In a small bowl, mix the water and vanilla. Add this to the almond meal to create a paste. Blend the rice syrup into the almond paste, and add the flour. Dust a cutting board with flour, and place the cookie dough onto it. The dough should be soft but slightly firm. Using your hands, press the dough to form a 12- to 14-inch long log, rolling back and forth to make the log smooth.

With a serrated knife, start at one end of the log, and slice a 1/4-inch thick round of cookie dough using the knife in a back and forth motion. Place the cookies on a cookie sheet lined with parchment paper. Continue slicing the dough until all the dough has been used. Decorating the cookies with a small square of chocolate (dark, milk, or white) adds visual appeal and great flavor. Break a chocolate bar into small squares, and press a piece into the center of the cookies. An almond looks nice in the center, too. Bake the cookies for about 20 minutes or until golden brown. Cool and store in a glass jar.

Variations:

- Any nut, or combination of nuts, can be substituted for the almonds.
- Using pecans gives the cookies a flavor that reminds me of Christmas.
- Cashews taste light and soft.
- Brazil nuts are tasty as well.
- Try different spices in place of the cinnamon. Cardamom with cashews is to dance for!

best balls ever!

best balls ever!

When I was twelve and my mom started to prepare healthier snacks for our family, she found this recipe somewhere. I remember after eating one of these balls, I felt fantastic. Years later, I began to search for quick and easy ways to incorporate superfoods into my family's treats. Remembering back to my childhood, I went to my old recipe box and pulled out this recipe. Below, you'll find the original version, called Original Best Balls, and these two variations: Fruity Best Balls and Peanut Butter Best Balls. If the superfoods I've listed are not available to you, use the Original Best Balls recipe, and swap some of the wheat germ (equal parts) for the superfoods you can find. It's a really fun recipe to play with, so however you mix them up, they will be chock-full of super goodness.

Original Best Balls

1/4 cup peanut butter
1/4 cup honey
1/2 cup wheat germ
1/4 cup raisins
1/4 cup sunflower seeds
Shredded coconut or chopped nuts for rolling balls

Mix all of the ingredients together, and shape small amounts of dough into balls. Roll them in coconut or chopped nuts. It's that simple!

Fruity Best Balls	Peanut Butter Best Balls
1/4 cup almond butter	1/4 cup peanut butter
1/4 cup honey (or other liquid sweetener)	1/4 cup honey (or other liquid sweetener)
1 tablespoon dried blueberries	1 tablespoon dried blueberries
1 teaspoon pure vanilla extract	1 teaspoon pure vanilla extract
1/8 teaspoon sea salt	1/8 teaspoon sea salt
1/4 cup Brazil nuts, chopped	1/4 cup Brazil nuts, chopped
1/3 cup rice bran solubles	1/3 cup rice bran solubles
1/3 cup shredded coconut	1/3 cup shredded coconut
1/2 teaspoon ground cinnamon	1/2 teaspoon ground cinnamon
1 teaspoon goji berry powder	2 teaspoons baobab fruit powder
1 teaspoon baobab fruit powder	1 teaspoon maca root powder
1/2 teaspoon acai powder	1 teaspoon lumca powder
1/2 teaspoon maqui berry powder	3 teaspoons sacha inchi powder
1/2 teaspoon maca root powder	
1/2 teaspoon lumca powder	
2 teaspoons sacha inchi powder	

Place the first six ingredients in a bowl and mix them well. In a separate bowl, combine the remaining dry ingredients and stir. Add the dry ingredients to the wet mixture, and stir to combine. With a spoon, scoop out some dough and shape it into a ball with your hands. Roll the balls in coconut or chopped nuts to cover. Continue this process until all the dough is used. These balls can be stored in an airtight jar and kept for two weeks. I keep these balls in my car for times when I need some extra nutrition or when family and friends need a boost. They are easy to bring anywhere and come in handy as a quick snack.

Variations:

- For a chocolate ball, replace the goji, maqui, acai, and dried blueberries with 1 teaspoon cocoa powder. Increase the maca and lumca to 1 teaspoon each, and add 1 tablespoon chopped dark chocolate.
- Play with different sweeteners (maple syrup, agave, or coconut nectar); nut butters (peanut butter or cashew butter); or superfoods (of which there are many). Keep the wet-to-dry ingredient ratios the same. That is, a dry ingredient should be replaced with an equal amount of another dry ingredient. As long as the ratio is kept the same, you can change out anything.

pecan pie

pecan pie

Pecan Pie anyone? This is my all-time favorite pie! I just love it served with whipped cream, and while I'm eating, my taste buds are dancing! I usually make this pie a couple of times a year, for Thanksgiving and Christmas. I make sure to prepare enough to last for a few days after each holiday.

3 cups pecans (Measure first. Then chop into fine or coarse pieces.)

3 tablespoons kudzu root powder (as a thickener)

1-1/4 teaspoons agar powder (a vegan gelling agent)

1/4 teaspoon sea salt

1-3/4 cups water

1 cup rice syrup

3/4 cup maple syrup

2 teaspoons pure vanilla extract

1 tablespoon coconut oil or butter

Pecan Pie is up there among my top, all-time favorite desserts. For this pie, I soak and dry pecans ahead of time. (See Soaked and Dried Nuts on page 77.) I keep a few types of nuts prepared this way on hand for cookies, breakfast cereals, snacks, etcetera. One can never have enough nuts.

Bake a 9-inch piecrust according to the package directions, or make your own. Spread the chopped pecans over the baked piecrust. Now prepare the filling.

Preheat the oven to 350 degrees. In a medium saucepan, combine all of the ingredients except the vanilla, coconut oil, and pecans. Mix well. Once the kudzu has dissolved, bring the liquid to a soft boil on medium heat, stirring continuously.

After the mixture thickens and becomes slightly translucent, turn the heat to low and let the sauce simmer for a few minutes. Turn off the heat, add the vanilla and coconut oil or butter, and mix well.

Pour the filling into the piecrust on top of the pecans. With a spoon, press any nuts that float to the top back into the filling. Bake the pie until the edges bubble slightly.

Remove the pie from the oven, and set it aside to cool. Don't worry if the filling is still a bit runny; this is normal. As the pie cools, the agar will set, and the filling will become solid. Once cooled, store the pie in the refrigerator.

Variations:

- You can use any nut you like in the pie.
- The filling for Pecan Pie tastes a lot like caramel, so you can use it to top off any dessert.
- Layer Chocolate Pudding (page 85), Almond Créme (page 89), and Pecan Pie filling in parfait glasses to make a fancy dessert. Because it takes time for each pudding to set, stagger their preparation times, so each layer cools completely in the parfait glasses before the next layer is added. If this seems like too much work, combine them together in a bowl and enjoy. Any of the combinations is a wonderful mix of favorite flavors.

Dancing
in the Kitchen

a word on breakfast

When I was growing up, there were many mouths to feed in the morning before school. There were eleven of us kids, plus my mom and dad. Mom often had a baby to take care of, so once we were old enough, we were trained by an older sibling to make breakfast for at least ten people. And mind you, we had to get ourselves ready for school as well. The five oldest kids, of which I was one, made breakfast for at least ten people once or twice a week.

Starting the evening before, we'd take butter out of the refrigerator to soften, move orange juice concentrate from the freezer to the refrigerator, and set the table for the morning meal. Back then, breakfast usually consisted of orange juice, toast, and oatmeal, scrambled eggs, or Cream of Wheat. Whoever was in charge of breakfast that morning got to choose the menu. Making toast for everyone would have taken all morning in a toaster, so older children taught younger siblings to put bread on a cookie sheet and toast it under the broiler.

One cookie sheet held twelve slices of bread, and we had to watch the bread closely so that it wouldn't burn. Halfway through toasting, we'd flip the slices to toast the other side. The softened butter spread easily and quickly onto the toast. If we forgot to put salt in the oatmeal or Cream of Wheat, no one would eat it. On those days, the cereal became dog food. When it was my turn to make breakfast, I was strictly instructed: "DON'T FORGET THE SALT." We all ate breakfast together, loaded our own dishes into the dishwasher, grabbed our books, and walked three-quarters of a mile to school.

My children don't have to make breakfast for everyone like I did because I love being in the kitchen. Breakfast is much easier to prepare for my small brood than for a family of thirteen. Still, I like breakfast to be simple. Back when I was getting three children off to school and I had many animals that needed to be fed, something easy and quick worked the best. I did as much preparation as I could the evening before to keep things moving smoothly in the morning. We all know that eggs and toast, dry cereal, smoothies, and yogurt are easy to make, but are there any other healthy options?

As mentioned earlier, Miso Soup (page 27) is a staple at our breakfast table. With the Clear Broth (page 25) already made, I just heat it up and add miso paste. Simple and easy. The salty flavor helps to ground my children after a night of rest, and the soup helps to bring them back from dreamland. With this in mind, I try to keep breakfast as savory as possible. Along with Miso Soup, I prepare many different types of soft grains such as rice, millet, quinoa, polenta (a.k.a. corn grits), and oats.

Usually the night before, I prepare enough grain for dinner, so I can use the extra for breakfast. In the morning, I add just enough water to cover the grain in a pot, turn on the heat, and allow it to simmer until it is soft and creamy. It isn't necessary to stay at the stove to watch the pot, so I'm freed up to help out wherever I'm needed. One thing I really like is that each bowl of grain can be garnished with whatever toppings each person wants: maple syrup, gomashio (Japanese sesame salt), coconut oil, roasted nuts or seeds, Almond Milk (page 79), ground flax seeds, soy sauce, butter, ghee and cinnamon, or fruit (fresh, frozen, or dried). Everyone is satisfied with their own concoction.

I serve dry cereal on days when we need to get out of the house extra early, and there isn't much time for grain to soften. I encourage you to do what works for you and your family. With four children, I didn't want to be making four different breakfasts each morning. So we had a meeting and came up with a breakfast plan. Each child got to pick their favorite breakfast, and one day a week I'd make each of those favorites. There was no arguing, and they were happy with this schedule. On weekends, I make pancakes or Japanese mochi, which is pounded sweet rice. These are two of our family favorites.

Now with only two children at home—one who has to get out the door to school and one who is homeschooled—breakfast is a bit easier. My older son drives himself to school, so that gives me more time in the kitchen to personalize breakfast. However you choose to prepare breakfast, remember it is the most important meal of the day. As my grandma used to say, "You want to have a breakfast that sticks to your ribs." You want breakfast to fuel your body and your brain. The easier you make this on yourself, the better the start of your day will be.

soft rice porridge

soft rice porridge

This is one of my most satisfying breakfasts. I love the creaminess of the rice, the richness of coconut oil, the crisp, fresh, sweet blueberries, the crunchy walnuts, and finally the smooth, delicious Almond Milk. It's a quick and easy breakfast, and my taste buds are satisfied with the tantalizing textures of each topping.

1/2 to 1 cup cooked brown rice per person
Water to cover the rice
1 to 2 teaspoons coconut oil
1 tablespoon ground flax or chia seeds
1/4 cup fresh blueberries or in-season fruit of your choice
Walnuts
Almond Milk (page 79)

Place the prepared rice in a saucepan, and add just enough water to cover it. Bring the ingredients to a boil. Reduce the heat, and allow the rice to simmer uncovered for about 15 minutes. When most of the water has been absorbed and the rice is soft and creamy, turn off the heat. Scoop the soft rice into bowls, and add the remaining ingredients.

millet apple porridge

millet apple porridge

I make a fabulous breakfast porridge with millet, apples, and cinnamon. This porridge can also be made the night before and poured into a glass baking dish to cool. In the morning, it can be cut and pan fried, just like Polenta (page 67). Topped with butter or coconut oil and walnuts, it's a perfect way to start the day!

- 1/2 cup millet, soaked 8 hours
- 2 cups filtered water (or half water and half apple juice for a sweeter taste)
- 1/8 teaspoon sea salt
- 1/2 teaspoon ground cinnamon
- 2 firm apples, peeled, cored, and diced into 1-inch cubes

Soak the millet overnight. In the morning, wash it several times, and drain the excess water. In a pot, combine the millet, water, salt, cinnamon, and apples. Bring to a boil, cover the pot with a lid, and reduce the heat to low, allowing the millet to cook for 30 minutes. Grab a spoon and a bowl, and savor this sweet, creamy morning porridge. Enjoy!

banana pancakes

banana pancakes

These pancakes make for a special breakfast! Or dinner. When I was a kid, we would occasionally have pancakes for dinner. Inevitably, one of my ten siblings would call out, "Pancake-eating contest!" I would always participate, even though I could never eat more than three. What I loved most was being with my sisters and brothers, cheering and laughing while we devoured pancakes.

1 egg
1 mashed banana
1 cup Almond Milk (page 79)
1/4 teaspoon sea salt
Dash of ground nutmeg
1/2 cup oatmeal, finely ground (Pulse grind in a coffee grinder or blender.)
1 to 1-1/2 cups flour
1 teaspoon baking powder

Preheat a skillet on medium heat. Whisk the egg in a bowl with a fork, and then add the banana, Almond Milk, salt, and nutmeg. Add the oatmeal and stir. In a separate bowl, stir together 1 cup of flour and the baking powder, and add this to the banana mixture. Stir lightly, folding in the remaining 1/2 cup of flour. If the batter is thin, add more flour to get the desired consistency.

When your skillet is hot to the touch, add a small amount of oil (coconut oil, butter, or olive oil). It may take several tries to learn how to avoid overheating the oil. Ladle some of the pancake batter onto the skillet. After a few minutes, use a metal spatula to check the underside of the pancake. If it's browned, flip the pancake to cook the other side. Continue making the pancakes until all of the batter is gone. Top them with butter, ground flax seeds, fresh fruit, nuts, or your favorite syrup. (We use warmed, pure maple syrup.) And, try them for dinner. I'm sure you and your family will love having breakfast for dinner!

Variations:

- To replace the egg, use flax seeds prepared this way: Grind 1 tablespoon of flax seeds into a fine meal using a coffee grinder. Place the flax meal into a bowl and add a scant 1/4 cup of boiling water. Stir and allow it to set for 10 minutes. Add this to the banana mixture in place of the egg.
- For apple pancakes, replace banana with 1/3 cup apple, peeled and finely grated. Replace the nutmeg with 1/4 teaspoon cinnamon.

maple nut crunch granola

maple nut crunch granola

When I worked in the deli of the first Jimbo's…Naturally! store, Jimbo loved the crumble I was making for the fruit crisps. One day, he asked if I would make just the topping for him. Being that he was a nice guy (and my boss), I made the topping. He passed it out to the employees, asking them for feedback. They gave it a big thumbs-up, so he asked me to make the topping in large quantities to sell as granola. He called the granola, "Jimbo's Maple Nut Crunch Granola." I used to joke with him about how his name got on MY granola. After almost thirty years, this granola is still popular in all five of our San Diego stores. Be careful: this granola is mouthwatering, crunchy, and delicious!

4 cups rolled oats
2 cups flour
1 cup almonds, chopped
1/4 teaspoon sea salt
1 teaspoon baking powder
1 cup maple syrup
1/3 cup oil
2 teaspoons pure vanilla extract

Preheat the oven to 350 degrees. In a large bowl, combine the dry ingredients. In another bowl, combine the wet ingredients. Pour the wet into the dry, and mix to coat all of the dry ingredients well.

Line a cookie sheet with parchment paper (optional). Spread the raw granola evenly onto the cookie sheet and into the corners as well. Place the cookie sheet on the middle rack in the oven to bake. If you have a convection oven, you can bake two cookie sheets of granola at a time. After 10 minutes, stir the granola well, moving the granola in the corners to the center of the cookie sheet and the granola from the center to the corners as best as you can. This will ensure that the granola cooks evenly. Every 5 minutes, stir the granola until it is golden brown. If you like a chunky granola, allow the chunks to stay together when you are stirring. If not, you can break them apart with a wooden spoon. When the granola becomes golden, remove it from the oven and cool. Storing it in glass jars keeps it fresh and crunchy.

Variations:

- Add different nuts or increase the amount of almonds.
- Add chocolate chips to the baked granola.
- Add dried fruit after baking, so the fruit doesn't dry out even more in the oven.
- Add dried fruit, ground flax seeds, fresh fruit, or nuts directly to your cereal bowl.
- Use the granola as a topping for ice cream or yogurt.

adaptations and transformations

When I was eighteen, I would occasionally babysit my younger siblings while my mom and dad traveled to Europe to ski cross-country races. Ski racing was something they took on as a personal goal, and it was an activity they could do together. I remember watching my mother prepare dinners for us in advance, taking notes on how she put this and that together to create our meals. My mom was an excellent cook, and I knew that one day I would have a family and would want to prepare these dishes for them. So I watched intently and learned all that I could. I would practice cooking for my younger siblings while my parents were out of the country, and my dishes turned out quite well. I had some blank recipe cards left in my recipe box from a high school Home Economics class, so I transferred all of my mom's recipes onto those cards and added them to the box. I still have the box with the original recipes inside.

Lo and behold, around age twenty-one, I became a vegetarian and have, for the most part, continued this way of eating ever since. So, what happened to all those great recipes in my old recipe box? They have been transformed into vegetarian versions of my mom's dishes, adapted to fit the requirements of how I want to feed my family. White flour, white sugar, and hydrogenated oils have been replaced with items I feel are a better fit for our lifestyle. I can't imagine my kitchen without the smells and tastes from my childhood. Part of dancing in the kitchen is reinterpreting what we learned as children and adapting it to fit our adult lives. Family recipes and memories are too precious to live without, even if your life takes another direction.

I hope this section inspires you to work with your favorite dishes and transform them into versions that meld past traditions with life in the present. I encourage you to make useful changes to family favorites. All of those beloved recipes can take on new life in your hands and continue on as favorites, while also fitting your tastes and nutritional needs.

I have adapted and transformed many recipes originated by others to fit my family's needs. We can never leave the best of the past behind; so much wisdom and good cooking would be lost.

When I was in middle school, I loved to bake! My favorite recipes were ginger snaps and my grandma's oatmeal raisin cookies. Because I made them often, I had most of the ingredients memorized and didn't need to look at the recipe cards. One summer afternoon, I was making oatmeal cookies and daydreaming while I added the ingredients to the bowl. My mind slipped from making oatmeal cookies to making ginger snaps, and I accidentally added molasses. I realized my mistake but was afraid to tell my mom.

I was frantic over what to do. I could throw everything out and start over, hoping nobody would notice, but I didn't want to waste what was already in the bowl. I confessed to my mom, and she encouraged me to continue on with the cookies and not to worry about the molasses. So I did. Well, these turned out to be the best cookies ever, so molasses was added as a permanent ingredient.

Fifteen years later, while working in the deli at Jimbo's…Naturally!, I decided to make my grandma's cookies for shoppers to buy and enjoy the same way I had as a child. Except, I had a new challenge now: many of the ingredients I used when I was young were not allowed in cookies sold at Jimbo's. Through trial and error, I created Grandma Duffy's Cookies without Crisco, white flour, or white sugar. I'm excited to share this recipe with you. You can keep it as it is or modify it to incorporate the flavors you love.

grandma duffy's cookies

grandma duffy's cookies

Here's to Grandma Duffy and her many recipes I use in carrying on family traditions. In addition to super-delicious cookies, this recipe gives my children a glimpse into my childhood, their great-grandmother's life, and their family history. What a perfect way to share memories.

In a bowl, mix together:

2 cups flour
2 cups oatmeal
1/2 teaspoon ground cloves
1/2 teaspoon ground cinnamon
2 teaspoons baking powder
1/4 teaspoon sea salt

In a separate bowl, mix together:

2 eggs, beaten with a fork
1/2 cup maple syrup
1/4 cup molasses
1/4 cup oil (light olive oil or coconut oil)
1/2 cup walnuts, chopped
1/3 cup raisins, plumped in water (Place raisins in 1 cup of hot water to plump them. Allow to cool, and then add the raisins and water to the bowl.)

Preheat the oven to 350 degrees. With the wet and dry ingredients in separate bowls, add the wet ingredients to the dry ingredients and mix well. Allow the dough to sit for 10 minutes, and then spoon the batter onto an oiled cookie sheet or one lined with parchment paper. You can choose to make small or large cookies; it's up to you. Bake until done.

soul soup

soul soup

I recall a late fall day when I was out riding a trail with Mecca after school. We were several miles from home when the sky became very dark. Sensing that a storm was coming, I did my best to engage Mecca to get us home quickly before the storm hit. About a mile from home, a heavy snow began to fall. Fortunately, the trail widened a bit, and I was able to canter Mecca, who easily obeyed the urging of my leg. By the time she was finally untacked and I was on my way to the house, I was freezing!

As I opened the door, I smelled something wonderful: my mom's vegetable soup and freshly baked bread. Have I mentioned that my mom is a great cook? I loved her vegetable soup. I fixed myself a slice of thick warm bread with butter and a large bowl of hot soup. I sat at the table, dunking my bread into the soup's broth, savoring every mouthful. I call my mother's soup "Soul Soup" because of how warm and nourished I felt eating it. Although my mom used a beef base in her soup, I created a vegetarian version that my family and I just love. That same warm, safe, and grounded feeling I felt on that blustery and snowy day is still mine each time I sip this soup. When I prepare a pot of Soul Soup, I'm transported back in time to the days of being young and carefree. I love you, Mom!

- 1 onion, diced
- 1 tablespoon olive oil
- 2 bay leaves
- 6 to 10 button mushrooms, washed, stems removed, and thinly sliced
- 1 to 2 medium potatoes, peeled and diced into 1-inch cubes
- 6 cups water
- 2 to 3 tablespoons tomato paste
- 1/2 teaspoon sea salt
- 3 to 4 medium carrots, sliced into 1/2-inch rounds
- 2 to 3 cups cauliflower flowerets (Try to make them the same size for even cooking.)
- 2 to 3 cups cabbage, cubed
- 1 cup frozen peas
- 1 large garlic clove, minced

In a large pot, sauté the onion in the olive oil. When the onion is translucent, add the bay leaves and mushrooms, stirring well. Next add the potatoes, pouring the water into the pot and bringing the soup up to a simmer. Now add the tomato paste and salt. Allow this to simmer for about 5 to 10 minutes before adding the carrots. After a few minutes, place the cauliflower into the pot, followed a few minutes later by the cabbage. Bring the soup back up to a simmer. After a few minutes, check the cauliflower. If it's about 50 percent cooked, add the peas and garlic. Now stir the pot gently and taste the broth. Adjust the flavor by adding more salt, garlic, or tomato paste. Let the soup simmer on low until the vegetables are cooked to the tenderness you like. Enjoy with some buttered bread, crackers, or just as it is, full of goodness and warmth.

yum

yum

In the summer, when we go to New York to visit Jimbo's side of the family, we are always greeted with a huge pot of Middle Eastern white rice, hummus, salmon, and vegetables. My mother-in-law, Yvette, makes many different types of delicious rice dishes that my family loves. One recipe of hers that I now make in our home is a rice dish that we call, "Yum." The very first time I walked into Jimbo's parents' house it had a smell that I had not experienced before. I came to know this scent as a combination of basmati rice, onion, tomato, and turmeric. One evening while we were visiting, Yvette made a one-pot meal that tasted out of this world. I asked her if she would explain how she put everything together. I am excited to share with you my version of Yvette's scrumptious one-pot meal. It doesn't take long to prepare this dish, and I'm sure that you will find that the name fits it perfectly: yummy Yum!

> 1 onion, diced
>
> 2 garlic cloves, minced
>
> 1 tablespoon olive oil
>
> 3 fresh shiitake mushrooms, thinly sliced
>
> 3 cups water
>
> 2 cups white basmati rice
>
> 1 potato, peeled and cubed
>
> 1 cup winter squash, cubed with skin and seeds removed
>
> 2 carrots, sliced into 1/2-inch rounds
>
> 1/2 teaspoon curry powder or turmeric
>
> 1 teaspoon sea salt
>
> 1 cup red chili beans, cooked and drained (See cooking instructions on page 33.)

In a warm pot, sauté the onion and garlic in the olive oil until the onion is translucent. Add the mushrooms, and sauté a few minutes more. Now add the water, and bring to a boil. While the water is heating, wash the rice several times and then drain it well. Once the water is boiling, add the potato, squash, carrot, curry, salt, and beans. Bring the ingredients back up to a boil, and add the rice, stirring it into the vegetables. One last time, bring everything up to a boil, place a lid on the pot, and reduce the flame to low.

Allow the rice to cook for 25 minutes. Remember, you can use a flame tamer to prevent the bottom of the pot from scorching. In the Middle East, the darkened rice at the bottom of the pot is considered a delicacy as well as the favorite part of the rice in Jimbo's family. When you remove the lid from the pot, you will see the contrasting colors—the yellow rice, the orange squash and carrot, the brown mushrooms, and the red beans. There is nothing more wonderful after a busy day than to have a tasty, lovely-looking dish—and with just one pot to clean after dinner.

serenity's chocolates

serenity's chocolates

I mentioned earlier that I have a small circle of women friends who meet regularly for tea. Serenity is one of these women who gather. She has many of the same goals that I do regarding food, and we share with each other the best ways to keep our families healthy. Serenity has also written a cookbook called Ginger, and in her book, she has a wonderful recipe for raw chocolates. I make these chocolates on a regular basis with some added flair of my own.

> 1/4 cup expeller-pressed coconut oil, melted
> 2 tablespoons maple syrup
> 3 tablespoons sifted cocoa powder
> 1 tablespoon raw cashew butter
> 1 teaspoon pure vanilla extract
> A pinch of sea salt

Combine all of the ingredients together in a bowl and mix well. Spoon the chocolate mixture into a candy mold. Place the mold in the freezer for 15 minutes to set the chocolate. Now pop the chocolate out of the molds. (They come out quite easily.) Place the chocolates in a jar and store them in the refrigerator. I keep many different jars with a variety of chocolate flavors in my refrigerator. My kids have these creamy, healthful chocolates available to them almost all the time to satisfy their sweet tooth.

Once you have all the ingredients and the molds, this recipe is as easy as one, two, three. After making these scrumptious chocolates many times, I found my own favorite variations.

Variations:

- Add 1/2 teaspoon of ground Turkish coffee or espresso to the chocolate mixture before spooning into the molds.
- Fill molds halfway with the chocolate mixture. Then add a small amount of roasted, chunky peanut butter, marshmallows, or chèvre cheese. Cover with more chocolate mixture to fill the molds.
- Add chopped nuts or dried fruits to the chocolate.
- Replace the vanilla with rum, and add finely chopped pecans (very delicious and fun for the holidays).

grandma duffy's fruitcake

grandma duffy's fruitcake

Fruitcake has gotten a bad rap! When I mention fruitcake, everyone makes a face, and a few run for the hills. I've tasted those fruitcakes, too, but MY fruitcake is not your typical fruitcake. It's more like the traditional version you would have found decades ago. About thirty years ago, I took on the challenge of creating a healthier version of my grandma's fruitcake, which used to resemble the Christmas versions with its bright red and green cherries. This recipe has gone through a major transformation. With more and more organic ingredients available today, Grandma Duffy's Fruitcake is 95% organic. I'm confident that if you like dried cherries (not the artificially colored red or green ones), dates, and raisins, you will love this traditional Christmas fruitcake!

For the past ten years, I've been sending a batch of fruitcake—minus one loaf for tasting—to my mom and dad in Wisconsin. They love it so much, and I'm honored to make it for them. Since I have been the one to carry on the family tradition of making fruitcake, family members who want a loaf or two find this Christmas delicacy in their mailboxes. It is happily sent from my house to theirs. The year before my grandma passed away, Mom and Dad took her one of my fruitcakes to get her feedback. She had been the master fruitcake maker for over fifty years, so they wanted to see if my version would pass her taste test. I'm delighted to announce that it did, and with flying colors.

I'm sharing this secret family recipe with the hope that it inspires you to start a tradition of your own. As the last recipe in my book, I'm honoring my grandma, Eva Sommerville Duffy, the earliest dancer in my family's kitchens who I had the privilege of knowing. Grandma, thank you for sharing this recipe with my mom so that the tradition of making fruitcake could be passed down to me. I can carry on the dance!

Grandma Duffy's Fruitcake (a.k.a. The Best Fruitcake in the World)

I start my preparation for fruitcake a couple of weeks before Thanksgiving, when the new crop of dried cherries shows up at our local farmers' market.

1 pound dried Bing cherries
Brandy or cognac (enough to cover cherries)

Place the cherries in a quart jar, filling it to the top with your choice of brandy or cognac. Secure the lid on the jar, give it a shake and then allow the cherries to soak up the alcohol for at least two weeks. Now you're ready to make fruitcake.

1 cup maple syrup	**1/2 teaspoon sea salt**
1-1/2 cups dates, pits removed and roughly chopped	**2 cups water**
1-1/2 pounds raisins	**3 oranges (zest only)**
1/2 cup oil (I use a light olive oil.)	**3 lemons (zest only)**
	3 eggs (whisked with a fork)

3 cups flour	2 teaspoons baking powder
1/4 teaspoon each: ground cloves, ground cinnamon, ground allspice, and ground nutmeg	2 cups walnuts (I use soaked and dried walnuts because they tend to be sweeter.)

The evening before making the fruitcake, place the syrup, dates, raisins, oil, salt, and water in a pot. Bring the mixture up to a boil, then reduce the heat to a simmer, and place a lid on the pot. Allow everything to cook for 20 minutes, stirring occasionally. Turn off the heat and let the mixture cool overnight.

In the morning, preheat the oven to 325 degrees, and place the cherries and brandy in a large bowl with the date mixture, the citrus zests, and the eggs. Mix very well.

Combine the flour, spices, and baking powder in a small bowl. Stir the flour mixture, along with the walnuts, gently into the wet ingredients. If the batter seems dry, add alcohol in small increments. Oil your baking dishes and then dust the inside with flour to coat the oil on the bottom and the sides.

I use different sizes of baking dishes (round and square) as well as small loaf pans so that I can give a loaf to my fruitcake-loving friends. This recipe fills about 8 small loaf pans or one regular-sized loaf pan.

Spoon the batter into a baking dish or loaf pan, filling it about three-quarters full. Place the baking dish on the oven's middle rack, and cook for about 1 hour. Depending on the dish size, the fruitcake may take more or less time to bake.

After 1 hour of baking, place a toothpick into the center of a loaf. If it comes out clean, the fruitcake is done. If not, continue baking until the toothpick comes out clean, without any wet batter on it.

Remove the fruitcakes from the oven, and allow them to cool completely before removing them from the baking dishes. When they're out of their baking dishes, wrap each loaf in parchment paper and put it into a plastic bag. I store my loaves in my refrigerator, and every time I open the door and see them there, I am reminded that the holidays have arrived!

Honestly, I don't wait until the loaves are cooled before slicing into one. I take my knife and serve myself a healthy portion, anticipating that first, familiar, fruity bite. As a child, I watched my mother eat her fruitcake with a slice of cheese on top, and now I do the same. With the cheese in place and a warm cup of tea, I take my first bite, savoring all the flavors that make up this traditional Christmas cake. Life is good!

keep dancing

It has been a privilege to share my story and my recipes—my dance—with you. In closing, I want to emphasize that I believe love is the answer to life's questions; it truly is! Love begins inside of you. It is imperative that you find a path that leads you there. The negative messages you've heard about who you are need to be removed, one at a time, and replaced with positive ones. I urge you to do what it takes to find your true love: yourself. If the recommendations in this book don't take you there, please do not give up until you find something that does. I guarantee that when you begin to love yourself, your life will change. Do what it takes to find your way back to yourself because if everything falls apart around you, you will always have your self-love to stand on. This is the way to true happiness.

I didn't like myself—let alone love myself—in the beginning of my journey. The abuse I inflicted upon my body could not have come from a place of self-love. When I began to look for someone to love me, someone to treat me well because I couldn't do that for myself, I was set up for failure. As a lost and lonely eighteen-year-old, I embarked on a twenty-year journey to find the love of my life, my knight in shining armor. Or maybe a fairy godmother who would wave her magic wand and create my "happily ever after." But then one day, I looked in the mirror and realized that all these years I had been searching for myself. I am my own hero. No one else can do the work that has to be done; it's up to me.

And so, I can now close this door as another one, I'm sure, will open. My journey to create a healthy relationship with food is over. I have arrived. I started off as a young adult, not sure of who I was and where my life was going, and along the way, I found myself. I would not wish one of my worst of times on anyone. Though the times were hard, I know that because of them, I have become who I'm supposed to be.

Writing this book has been a journey in and of itself, painful at times, as I revisited memories that have been asleep for many years. However, the desire to share my story and to share my quest for a healthy relationship with food was stronger than the fear of old memories. So as the door closes gently and slowly behind me, I stand on the other side, treasuring the bittersweetness that is life. Everything I learned on the other side of that door has prepared me for what lies ahead—the savory and sweet, the richness of life and love. I wish you great joy, and as you consider your own relationship with food and try my recipes, please know that they are filled with love and best wishes for you along your path. I know you will find your way. May we all discover the joy of dancing in our kitchens, and may that joy help us dance gracefully through our lives. My best to you on your journey.

Namaste,
Colleen

acknowledgments

I'm so full of gratitude! To recover completely from anorexia and bulimia is a huge accomplishment and one I don't take for granted. Where would I be today without all of the beautiful people who've shared my life's journey? I've felt fear, rejection, courage, acceptance, deceit, joy, despair, and love. Thank you to each and every one of you who showed up in a way that brought me to a place where I could experience all of these emotions. Because of you, I've chosen which road to travel, which doors to open, and which to close. I am who I am today because of you.

Many of my dear friends and family members have participated in one way or another to help "birth" *Dancing in the Kitchen*. With a very full heart, I thank you. Laura Butler, this book would not have been written without your gentle nudge to get my story told. Even when I became distracted, I could hear the encouraging sound, *wuh-psh*, through the phone. Julie Wheaton, your wisdom, knowledge, and unwavering enthusiasm in preparing this book for publication are heartfelt. Your respect for my voice meant my story was told in my words. Suzanne, Shawn, Brigid, Shannon, Shelley, Karen, and Susan, you always listened to my latest inspirations for the many sections in this book. You read and listened attentively, always giving your honest feedback. Peggy, I'm grateful that you're walking alongside me on the journey to becoming conscious beings and living in present-moment awareness. Carol and Tom Duffy, there are no words that can express the depth of how much you both mean to me. It is a feeling that only the heart knows. I love you both so much! Jimbo, thank you for allowing me the space to become who I am, for loving me all those years, and for being a lighthouse so that I could find my way back home. The journey hasn't always been an easy one, but I know through love and commitment, we find our way. Joshua, Michael, Noah, and Sara, wow! Life is full of treasures, and you are my diamonds. Thank you for the opportunity to experience motherhood and to know the most powerful love of all: unconditional love.

FREE BOOK
WITH $100
PURCHASE